SEDUCTION

SEDUCTION

Tempt, Tease and Tantalize Your Lover

SNOW RAVEN STARBORN

SOURCEBOOKS CASABLANCA™
AN IMPRINT OF SOURCEBOOKS, INC.®
NAPERVILLE, ILLINOIS

This publication is designed to provide accurate and authoritative information in regard to the subject matter covered. It is sold with the understanding that the publisher is not engaged in rendering legal, accounting, or other professional service. If legal advice or other expert assistance is required, the services of a competent professional person should be sought.—*From a Declaration of Principles Jointly Adopted by a Committee of the American Bar Association and a Committee of Publishers and Associations*

Trademarks: All brand names and product names used in this book are trademarks, registered trademarks, or trade names of their respective holders. Sourcebooks, Inc., is not associated with any product or vendor in this book.

Published by Sourcebooks, Inc.
P.O. Box 4410
Naperville, Illinois 60567-4410
(630) 961-3900
FAX: (630) 961-2168
www.sourcebooks.com

Starborn, Snow Raven.
　　Seduction: tempt, tease, and tantalize your lover/by Snow Raven Starborn.
　　　　p.cm.
　　ISBN 1-57071-833-4 (alk. paper)
　　1. Sex instruction for women. 2. Seduction. 3. Sexual fantasies. 4. Sexual
　　　excitement.
　　I. Title.

HQ46 .S85 2001
613.9'6—dc21

2001032269

Printed and bound in the United States of America
UG 10 9 8 7 6 5 4 3 2 1

Dedication

To Leo: my love, my king, my playmate, my best friend, and my cutie pie.

Table of Contents

Introduction

We love what we are. We are women. We love the way we move,
the way we look, the way we walk, and, of course, the way we talk.
We are the very definition of expression and style, and this
makes us powerful. We can win any fight. We can make
light of any darkness. We can seduce any man.

We use color and fragrance and texture and motion as our
language to let the world know who we are and how we feel.
This is an advantage that will always be ours. And we love it.

This book is meant for you, whether you are young or mature,
single or married, gay or straight. Do whatever it is that makes
you happy, and love it, and taste it, and run your fingers over it,
and breathe it in. Enjoy everything that you want to enjoy,
even everything that you think you may want to enjoy.
May you have fun with yourself and with your love for others.
May you laugh, sing, love, and be loved.

Let no one tell you not to eat with your hands, or when to wear
open-toed shoes, or whether or not to hug your male friends, or
how long you should wait to call. All that matters is what your
heart tells you, and that you keep it full of joy and honesty.

May life tickle you like a feather.

Part One

Achieving Your Own Perfection

*T*he key to looking sensual is feeling sensual. By this I do not necessarily mean sexy. You can be sensual and have absolutely no intention of having sex. That need not be your goal to enjoy sensuous moments and sensations. Your goal is to know yourself as beautiful. It is to run your fingers over your lips and enjoy it more than you would a kiss. Feel your hair moving; allow its gentle sway to tickle you; slide your foot over the bare skin of your leg; feel the neat shape of your knees.

Keep everything in your life simple—from dress to hair to makeup to any accessories. Use only what you know looks good. You will always feel gorgeous. The fewer pieces of jewelry you wear the better, and the clothing you wear should be something that has good feelings or memories for you.

Above all, you should be comfortable—do not wear anything in which you feel restrained. If you want to bend down and pick up a shell on the beach, you must be able to. If you want to slip off your shoes and swish your toes in a fresh puddle, you must be able to as well. Never wear anything that does not please you, even if it pleases your date. Dress for you.

Makeup should almost be nonexistent—use foundation only where you need it (under the eyes and to cover blemishes is fine), and use a shade to match your skin tone. Use a tiny amount of brown powder to line your eyes. Curl your eyelashes only (it is never prudent to wake up looking like a raccoon, and then have to go scurrying off to the washroom to remove migrating mascara). Use a berry liner to lightly line and fill in your lips, and a bit of powder for the nose and forehead only. You'll feel fresh and radiant and you may find yourself using the look every day. A quick pinch of the cheeks will bring up the perfect blush.

Perfume your hair as the fragrance will linger longer, and you will learn to know your hair for its own sexuality. It has a personality all its own. Try less to control it, and let it show you its waves and fun little flips. You may want to have your hair professionally done for the night. Ask for a soft feel and try waves if you normally straighten it, and vice versa. Keep the style for several days if you can. The memory of your fantastic date will stay with you and you will feel gorgeous and glamorous.

Have your meal at a small table for two. You can use a coffee table with floor cushions to sit on for this purpose. There are many gorgeous little patio tables on the market now that are the perfect size for private dinners and have exotic decorations. It is well worth the money to buy one. Eating close enough to feed each other arouses deep conversation.

Brush your teeth and floss just before the date as well as after dinner. You'll feel like smiling a lot more. If you cannot afford one of the new laser teeth-whitening treatments, invest in a gentle bleaching treatment for your teeth, and use it regularly. However, even if you need to save the money for six months, it will be worth every penny to get the treatment done. The treatments are easy, quick, and very effective. The effects also last for years. I cannot stress enough the importance of white teeth. You'll smile more every day and that will make you happier. It sounds silly and psychological, but it really, truly works. You will look tanner, your complexion will look more even, and you will look healthier.

Do not overdo the perfume. A simple dab of essential oil on the pulse points is all you ever need (men find it less suffocating). If you like to use a specific perfume, use only that one (like a signature scent). By lightly misting your hair, the scent will last longer. Remember: if you can smell your own perfume, you're wearing too much.

The Lingerie Cabinet

This is the best part of getting dressed. The truly sensual woman has an entire chest of drawers devoted to lingerie and the like. This cabinet should be a thin, graceful, vertical cabinet with many small drawers. One with a top that flips up to reveal jewelry and perfumes and scarves (handcuffs?) is very handy.

All the lingerie should be very well made. Fine lingerie is very expensive, so only buy pieces when you can afford them. There is no sense in going into debt for underwear. Most importantly, wear what works for your body. You need not waste money on clingy garters with tight straps if you honestly look better in a satin chemise. This is where you really get to have fun. The right undergarment will make you feel like a goddess. Only wear what you feel great in, even if you don't think anyone else will ever see it.

Don't limit lingerie to clothing. A dainty ankle bracelet can also be lingerie if it is primarily hidden from view. Only the watchful eye will get to see it, and that perceptive person will feel privileged. Wearing delicate little black pearl earrings while wearing your hair down is an easy way to feel sensual. You may be the only person who knows you are wearing them, but your little secret will give you a raw, feminine power.

If you know your gentleman very well, or are married, let him pick out the lingerie himself. Let him look through the many drawers, and perhaps you will leave a poem in one of them. If you are married, encourage your man to try boxer shorts in soft fabrics and sexy colors. They are infinitely more sensual around the house than old shorts and a T-shirt. Purchase a nice, small dresser for him made of a dark wood. Place cedar cutouts inside to lightly scent his boxers, socks, and ties, and help him keep everything inside folded and washed with care. He will become an organized man who takes good care of himself. That makes a man confident and sexy.

Bench Pressing Your Healthy Sexuality

Nothing is sexier than a healthy woman, and you do not have to be very strong or muscular to look healthy and sexy. To enhance the work you have done to look your best, try one of the skin-firming creams that are sold by reputable vendors. They actually do work with daily use, and every little bit helps.

By exercising for only a few minutes a day and an additional few minutes right before the date, your muscles will look shapely and you will look statuesque. Stretching will relax you and make you feel more confident. Make sure to always maintain good posture as well, and check yourself often. By simply standing up straight you will appear thinner and taller. Your stomach will look flatter and your chest will look bigger.

Above all, be proud of your body, and remember to wear your nipples as though they are jewelry. Almost all women have nipples that are uneven or different from each other. The only person who will ever notice this is you.

You should relax and soothe every tight and sore area every day. Do not allow pain and tension to build up. Simply lie flat on your bed with a pillow under your knees and slowly relax every little part of your body, one area at a time. Do this right after work before you begin any other activity. This will rejuvenate you and give you more energy. Massage your neck and shoulders with a mild lotion and slowly roll your head around in a circle, first in one direction, then the other.

Use these simple stretches whenever you need to. Just imagine the well-being and strength you'll exude as you greet your date. Do not obsess over your curves. You may think that you are imperfect—he does not. He thinks you are gorgeous. If you simply carry yourself proudly and confidently, everyone will see you as beautiful, just as he does. You are his goddess, behave appropriately.

Hip Stretch

Lie on your back with your knees bent. Place your left foot on your right thigh, with your left thigh resting open. Pull your right thigh toward your chest for twenty to thirty seconds. Then alternate. Do this three times on each side.

Inner Thigh Stretch

Sit on the floor with your legs in a V position. Curl your toes back toward you. Slowly stretch your upper body forward and try to touch your toes. Do not bend your knees, and do not overstretch yourself. Do not bounce your body to try to get further down. Stretch for thirty seconds, then come back up.

Squats

Stand up with your feet about shoulder width apart, and your arms straight out in front of you. Bring your hips and butt back and bend your knees forward, no farther than your toes. Then straighten your legs. Repeat twenty times.

Dips

Sit on a chair against the wall. Hold the front of the chair with your hand. Bend your elbows at a 90 degree angle, lower your body, then push back up, keeping your back straight. Repeat twenty times.

Buttock Crunches

Whenever you are standing in line, sitting, or looking into a store window simply squeeze your buttocks together. Do ten times per set. Try to do this at least fifty times every day, and your rear end will thank you in many ways.

A Chant Just for You

Say this chant before you have a date, an interview, or any occasion when you may need a little extra help feeling like the goddess you know you are. Give yourself a few minutes to really let it sink in, and repeat it if necessary. You must be totally aware of and in love with yourself. Remember your accomplishments, triumphs, and wonderful, wonderful little quirks that turn the world on.

"There is no one like me. I am the only person who does little things in a certain way. That's what he likes about me. That's what I like about myself."

• Dab pulse points with appropriate oil or perfume.

• Stand in front of your mirror.

• Stand straight with your shoulders back, chest out, chin up, stomach slightly tensed.

- Close your eyes and start to breathe in through your nose, out through your mouth, sighing on the exhale.
- Clear your mind of all thoughts. Think of a blank white page.
- Let yourself breathe and relax.
- Repeat the breathing exercise three times.
- Now, open your eyes a little and lift your chin slightly as if facing a gentle wind.
- Slowly run your fingers through your hair, touching your scalp, all the way back.
- Look at your face—the hollow under your cheekbones, the softness of your lips.
- Pout a little, then smile, and admire how you look.
- Lightly pinch your cheeks for color and smile at yourself in total peace.
- You are beautiful!

Lobster and Lace: Plans for Complete Seduction

Within the following chapters you will learn how to fully love and appreciate yourself. Each chapter is one seduction. Make them your own and live them. These seductions continue along a sensual progression and each theme is fun and different. Each seduction includes the following:

- A steamy poem, which you are encouraged to claim as your own or change to suit you. You may also want to try writing your own poem—you'll be amazed and delighted at the effects the poetry has on your date.
- A designated activity for the two of you to participate in and complete notes on how to enjoy that activity.
- The perfect essential oil to use on pulse points or to delightfully scent your home, with instructions on how to mix essential oils to create the perfect scent.
- How to set the surroundings and get into the mood.
- A menu for the date, and suggestions in the way of food and drink, including scrumptious cocktails and nonalcoholic alternatives.
- A morning-after-the-date recipe so that the seduction continues well into the next day.

Part Two

The Seductions

The Very First Seduction

Poem
"You Noticed How I've Been Looking at You"

Activity
Palm-Reading Session

Pulse Point Oil
Ginger Flower

Color Scheme
Deep Green

Menu
Take-out Sushi,
Hot and Sour Soup,
Fresh Endive Salad,
Mango Ice Cream with Lychees, and
Hot Sake or Cucumber Infusion

The Morning After
Japanese Breakfast Dim Sum
or Papaya and Coconut Sticky Rice,
and Hot Green Tea

You Noticed How I've Been Looking At You

Crumple me as you would a piece of paper; blank, white.

Cover me with words that you wouldn't let anyone see

and then rip me apart and scatter me over your body,

knowing that I would fold up and let anyone know.

Write your words, wants, passions, and mad desires

that drive you to a pulsing need.

Curse me with your blood as you write magic things.

Use me to slice your skin and draw more so you may continue.

Then tear me as you would an enemy

and burn me so no one will ever see what you wrote.

Rub me as dust over your body

and massage into me your hardness.

Make me moist with your sweat so I slide over your skin

easily and slowly and pierce me so I'll glide with you.

*O*bviously, if you feel comfortable giving this poem you have no reservations, so you can use any and all of these sexy pointers that you desire. Let your passion be your guide and don't be afraid to have all the fun that the night has to offer you. This poem will definitely get him ready for you, and he will be begging to touch you by the time he is finished reading it. You will be performing a palm-reading session on him tonight, so maybe let him try to read your palm as well. Women are far more intuitive than men in most cases, so your reading of him will be far more exact.

Setting the Scene

Serve the meal on dark, Oriental-style dishes, and use chopsticks for fun. Place a large bowl in the middle of the table, fill it with water, and then place floating candles and flower blooms on the water's surface. Go to a fine fabric store and purchase a large piece of Oriental printed satin for use as a tablecloth or table runner. To make preparations for Asian-style dinners easy, you may wish to simply buy some large Oriental printed pillows with tassels and embroidery. Place these pillows on the floor and eat on the coffee table. Many exotic candleholders make excellent sushi plates. Simply make sure that they are not coated with harmful paint or other substances. Chill glass plates or candle holders in the freezer briefly before adding the sushi, as sushi is tastier when it is thoroughly chilled. Wear a kimono in a dark, sexy, ivy green. This is a very passionate color and is also a slimming color, being very dark. Dressing in one color all the way down is also very slimming, so buy a long dress, preferably with long sleeves. Trousers and a turtleneck sweater work well for this evening as well. Put your hair up and secure it with a chopstick. Another wonderful effect is to put your hair up in a bun with some bobby pins, thread some large pearls onto a needle and thread, and sew them loosely into your bun. Sew in one, pull the needle through your hair, add another pearl, and continue. This is very easy to do but looks very difficult.

Pulse Point Oil

GINGER FLOWER

For Ginger Flower oil, combine ginger oil with a few drops cucumber oil, and a drop or two of tuberose or hyacinth. Mix well and let sit overnight to marry the scents. Add an equal amount of jojoba oil if using pure essential oils and dot on your pulse points and behind the knees.

How to Serve the Poem

The poem should be prepared as soon as you feel attracted to a man and sense reciprocation. Write it with a brush-style Japanese calligraphy pen and black or dark green ink on a plain piece of rice paper, made for that purpose. Give it to your date as soon as he accepts your invitation or you accept his.

Menu

TAKE-OUT SUSHI, HOT AND SOUR SOUP, FRESH ENDIVE SALAD, MANGO ICE CREAM WITH LYCHEES, AND HOT SAKE OR CUCUMBER INFUSION (NONALCOHOLIC)

Sushi has a subtle, delightful flavor and is very sensual to eat. If you do not care for the taste of raw fish, there are many kinds of sushi that are vegetarian or have cooked shrimp, fish, and chicken in them. The hot and sour soup and endive salad will contrast with and round out the sushi, and the sweet/tart mango ice cream dessert will leave your palates thrilled. The taste of Sake takes getting used to, but many people develop a love for it, or you can substitute an alcohol-free refreshing cucumber infusion to drink.

Activity

PALM READING

Here is a chart if you would like to memorize some of the rudiments of palm reading. Read only his right hand (the left hand is used by professional palmists to clarify information only). Hold his hand gently in your left hand, and stroke his entire palm two or three times with your whole palm to get his whole body tingling. Then, using the tip of your right index finger, trace the lines on his hand and murmur your interpretations.

The Head Line determines mental capabilities and perceptions. If you see a deep, dark line tell him that he is determined and strong in his beliefs and his confidence in himself. If the line is thin and unpronounced, tell him you see that he thoroughly explores his options before committing. For a broken line, you might want to tell him that he will have many changes in his lifetime.

The Heart Line indicates how he deals with love and relationships. For a deep, unbroken line, say that he is sure in his decisions with his love life, and devoted to his partner. For a thin line, tell him he is a lady's man. For a broken line tell him that he may have a number of loves before he settles down.

The Life Line indicates the type and quality, but not the length of the life. If you see a long, straight, deep line, tell him he maintains his life and surroundings very well and is basically happy and successful. For a thin line tell him that he will do many exciting things and see many exciting places. If you see a broken line, tell him he is on a search for happiness in the here and now.

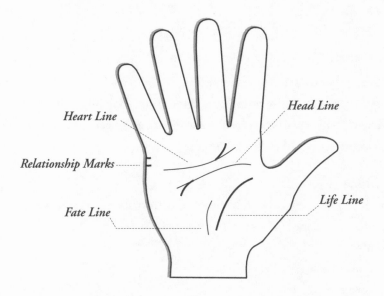

Heart Line

Head Line

Relationship Marks

Fate Line

Life Line

The Fate Line indicates your destiny and how well you use your talent. For a deep line, tell him that he will easily find his true calling. A thin short line indicates that he will want to develop his talents with many years of experience.

Relationship Marks indicate the relationships that will greatly affect the individual. Sometimes this interesting little mark can be right on. There will be one or more deep, noticeable lines. This may mean a lover, a best friend, a parent, or children. Wouldn't it be great if both of you had only one deep line each in the same place? That may mean that you were destined to be lovers forever.

The Morning After
Japanese Breakfast Dim Sum or Papaya and Coconut Sticky Rice, and Hot Green Tea

Go to a local market the day before and purchase a good selection of tasty dim sum–style items. There are many different kinds and most are very delicious. Arrange the food early in the morning and heat the items that need to be served warm. Several need to be steamed to release their best flavors, but this step is simple and only takes a few minutes. If these items are unavailable to you, make the morning extra special by preparing sweet and sticky papaya and coconut sticky rice. Serve hot green tea as you both greet your first morning together.

RECIPES

Take-out Sushi

Order fresh sushi from a good Japanese restaurant. Get a good selection of the many kinds that are available. When you arrive at home, arrange the sushi on square dishes or wooden sushi box platters. Have small sauce bowls for the soy sauce, and place little mounds of wasabi and pickled ginger on the corner of each serving tray.

Hot and Sour Soup

Many find this soup very seductive, as it is exotic and spicy but also somewhat sour. It is pleasing and teasing to the palate.

4 12-oz cans chicken stock
½ cup shredded bamboo shoots
½ cup thinly sliced mushrooms
1 tsp dark soy sauce
½ tsp sugar
1 tsp salt
½ tsp ground white pepper
2 ½ tbsp vinegar
2 tbsp cornstarch
3 tbsp water
1 pad soft bean curd (tofu), cut into thin strips
1 egg, lightly beaten
1 tsp sesame oil
4 tbsp chopped scallions

Place mushrooms, stock, and bamboo shoots in a saucepan. Bring to a boil and simmer for 10 minutes. Add the soy sauce, sugar, salt, pepper, and vinegar. Combine the cornstarch with the water. Add a little of the hot soup to the cornstarch, return to the pan, and heat to boiling, stirring constantly.

Add the bean curd and cook for 2 minutes. Just before serving, turn off the heat, add the egg, and stir a few times in a circular motion (one direction only). Add the oil and stir. Ladle into small Chinese soup bowls and garnish with the scallions.

Fresh Endive Salad

5 heads of endive
½ cup fresh walnuts, whole or broken
2 firm sweet apples
juice of 1 lemon
5 tbsp olive oil
salt

Cut the end off of the endive, chop into bite-size pieces. Rinse thoroughly in cold water, shake dry, place in a salad bowl, and sprinkle with walnuts. Core, then peel the apples and cut into very thin slices. Add apples to salad bowl and sprinkle with lemon juice. Toss. Add oil and salt and toss again. If desired, add more oil and salt. Serve immediately.

Mango Ice Cream with Lychees

1 mango, peeled, seeded, and roughly chopped
1 papaya, peeled, seeded, and roughly chopped
1 tbsp lemon juice
4 egg yolks
½ cup icing sugar
¾ cup whipping cream, whipped
1 can lychee fruits

Puree mango and papaya with lemon juice, set aside. Combine egg yolks and icing sugar in the top of a double boiler. Whisk until eggs are lemon color and thick. Remove from the heat and continue whisking another two minutes. Fold fruit puree into egg mixture. Blend in cream. Stir in drained, halved lychees. Pour into decorative four-cup mold and freeze five hours or overnight.

To remove, dip the mold into warm water for thirty seconds and invert onto a serving dish.

To serve, cut into thin slices with a sharp knife that has been run through hot water. If you prefer you can scoop it out as ice cream balls, but the slices are more unique.

Papaya and Coconut Sticky Rice

1 cup Japanese rice
½ cup sliced, fresh papaya

¼ cup shredded coconut
¼ cup coconut milk

Cook rice according to directions, adding ¼ cup less water than requested, replacing with coconut milk. Add papaya and shredded coconut. Pack tightly into small bowls and refrigerate for at least thirty minutes. When ready to serve, microwave for one minute and spoon out onto small plates. Garnish with a little extra coconut, and maybe a leftover lychee.

Sake

Be wary of drinking too much sake as it is highly alcoholic. Make sure that it is served very hot and preferably in a small ceramic carafe with tiny ceramic cups specifically made for the purpose. The carafe of sake can be microwaved on 20-second bursts if it gets cold, or you can use a plug-in style mug warmer on the corner of the table.

Cucumber Infusion

As an alternative to sake, create a cucumber infusion by adding many thin slices of cucumber to cold water. This is a very soothing drink and it will clear the palate for the next bite and help cool your tongue after the wasabi.

Dreamy Kisses Seduction

Poem
"Would You Like to Kiss Me?"

Activity
Kisses in the Kitchen

Pulse Point Oil
Neroli

Color Scheme
Platinum

Menu
Individual Chocolate Soufflés
with Raspberry Sauce,
and Chocolate Sodas or
Chocolate Milk (nonalcoholic)

The Morning After
Omelette for Two

Would You Like to Kiss Me?

If our lips were to meet, would yours touch back?

Would your hand reach up to stroke my cheek and neck or

would you simply stand, not moving away but not moving in?

Would you tangle your fingers in my hair and pull

me in for a deeper kiss?

Would you feel shock if I slid my hands around your waist and

up your back as you kissed me?

If you felt that you wanted to

tease my mouth with your tongue would you do it?

I will not kiss you first for fear that you would recoil.

I'll hide the nervousness in my stomach as I do

every time you walk by,

and every time I wonder:

if our lips were to meet,

would yours touch back?

*T*his is a very flirtatious seduction, but is not too involved. You are not revealing your emotional insecurities or your feelings yet. This is the seduction in which you will reveal only how magnificent you are. Be proud of who you are. He will see you as unique, a bright star, a great woman, a great temptation.

Setting the Scene

Keep your decorations and tableware simple for this evening. Metal or iron accessories for the home are very chic and show good taste. Dark stone dishes and darkly stained glasses are seductive without being flirty and girlish. A dim room with thick-leafed plants and dark red, filmy curtains skirting across the floor in the light evening wind are effective in creating a dream sequence. Wear something metallic but not flashy. A platinum velvet skirt works well, or a shimmery cotton sheath dress. Deep platinum, wide-leg, leather pants do wonders for your self-image. Position a quiet fan right outside the window to create the smooth wind if there isn't any. A trickling table fountain will make the perfect background noise. This evening's dessert is to be served by the light of many candles.

Pulse Point Oil

Neroli

Neroli is a tried and true blend. It is available at most shops that carry essential oils. It quickly becomes a favorite of most who try it. Apply neroli oil to your pulse points only. It is a strong scent and should be used sparingly. Dilute with jojoba to soften the scent. You may also wish to layer it under your signature scent. I like to add a teaspoon or so to my shower gel. It perks up whatever scent it is infused with.

How to Serve the Poem

Compose your own poem, or use the one at the beginning of the chapter. Place a bunch of narcissus (or paper-whites) on the table or coffee table and slip the poem on a small, white card among the petals (put his name on it, then send him over to smell the flowers—narcissus are a very addictive scent). All year long it is great to purchase narcissus bulbs at a garden store and place them right-side-up in a wide, shallow bowl resting on marble or rocks with water just reaching the roots of the bulbs. This is called forcing bulbs. Check the water daily and keep them in indirect sunlight, and in six to eight weeks you will have gorgeous, fragrant narcissus for your enjoyment.

Menu

INDIVIDUAL CHOCOLATE SOUFFLÉS WITH RASPBERRY SAUCE, AND CHOCOLATE SODAS OR CHOCOLATE MILK

The soufflés are sweet and seductive in their deep chocolate nature, but they are small, neat, and show uncommon good taste. They are not motherly like a chocolate cake; they are modern and delightfully sinful. So are you.

Activity

KISSES IN THE KITCHEN

Invite him into your home while the soufflés are in the oven. He will be given the chance to see you in action (now that the messy part is over), and even help. You will be making the chocolate sauce at this time. He will want to help—chocolate is, after all, a powerful aphrodisiac, and the smell of it will arouse him. When the moment is right, lick the chocolate sauce spoon (or offer it to him to lick), then lean forward and give him a lingering kiss. After he gets over his surprise, talk to him about what dessert items you like the most and then discuss what wonderful things you could do with those treats. Could you eat them off of each other's bellies, use them as body paint, or feed them to each other with your hands? Maybe you will feel inspired to use the raspberry sauce for your own creative pleasure. That is, of course, your objective for the evening. You shall become one with your dessert, and each other. Get silly and sexy; this sauce is quite irresistible. Indulge accordingly.

The Morning After

OMELETTE FOR TWO

Please! No more cake! Go out to a tiny café, your treat. The day is yours, so take charge. Order an omelette for two and fresh squeezed orange or guava juice. Plan the afternoon. Perhaps you will go to an old bookstore and look for valuable first editions.

RECIPES

Individual Chocolate Soufflés

6 oz bittersweet chocolate, chopped

1½ tbsp unsalted butter

2 tsp instant coffee

2 egg yolks

3 egg whites

3 tbsp dark rum, or rum-flavored extract

3 tbsp sugar

3 tbsp heavy cream

Raspberries and powdered sugar for garnish

Heat oven to 375° F. Butter two small ramekins (small, ceramic soufflé cups), and dust each with sugar. Melt half the chocolate over a double boiler; add the instant coffee and one tablespoon of the sugar. Add the rum, stir until smooth, and remove from the heat. Let cool for five minutes, then whisk the yolks in, one at a time.

In another bowl, beat the egg whites and a pinch of salt until they begin to form soft peaks. Add the sugar a bit at a time, until the mixture begins to form stiff peaks. Fold one-fourth of the egg mixture into the chocolate mixture, and then gently fold in the rest. Divide the batter between the two ramekins, place in the middle of the oven, and bake for seventeen minutes or so, until a toothpick comes out clean (remember that it is always better to slightly undercook a chocolate cake than to overcook it). Let cool for five minutes.

While they are baking, melt the rest of the chocolate in the double boiler; add the remaining one-half tablespoon of butter and heavy cream and whisk until smooth. Pour half of the sauce onto the dessert plates, run a knife around each of the ramekins, and invert a cake onto each plate. Top with raspberry sauce and powdered sugar and surround with raspberries.

Raspberry Sauce

Make this sauce the day before to add to the dessert plates.

1 cup fresh raspberries

½ cup sugar

1 tbsp cornstarch
1 tbsp lemon juice
1 tbsp cognac

Mix raspberries with sugar and heat, stirring frequently, to a boil. Press raspberries through a sieve to remove seeds (sieves can be purchased at any fine cooking store). Add more sugar if needed. Mix the cornstarch with the lemon juice and cognac. Heat the raspberry puree to a boil, stir in the cornstarch mixture, and cook, stirring, until thickened. Cool and use as desired on any dessert, fruit, or body part. Will keep in the fridge for two weeks.

Chocolate Soda or Chocolate Milk (nonalcoholic)
In a tumbler combine:
Ice
1 ½ oz Kahlua
½ oz cream
Fill with coke (pour coke quickly, it will mix the drink)

Serve chocolate milk as a nonalcoholic alternative.

I'll Say It for the First Time

Poem
"I Love You"

Activity
Train Ride

Pulse Point Oil
Yellow Rose

Color Scheme
Simple, Quiet Sky Grays

Menu
Cucumber Sandwiches and
Lemon Cream Sodas or
Lemon Sodas (nonalcoholic)

The Morning After
Wake and Dine in Another City

I Love You

I hold my breath to your neck, and a strained whisper

"I love you," rises up in my throat.

Should I say it?

Would you hear me?

Or would my voice crack in hunger for your reply?

I want to tell you again,

my cheek on your chest, and

wish you would say something back.

Something soft yet urgent, and

I want to answer you with a kiss,

feast on your lips and tongue and

move against you.

*T*his seduction is pure and charming. It will pave the way for amazing things to come. You have shown him that you are amazing, you have vision, and you are caring and deep and funny. Now you will show him that you have an untamable spirit and lust for adventure. Now you will tell him that you love him for the first time. Compared to you, there could never, ever, be an equal.

Setting the Scene

Ask him where he would like to go, and plan your train trip accordingly. Go to the country if he is from a more rural area or go to an exciting city where you can explore things all night and retire to your hotel in the early, cool light of morning. You will know where to go. Make sure you get a train that has private sleeping cars, in which you will be spending the length of the trip. You need not sleep overnight in the car; you only need to spend about four hours in it. Send him his ticket in the mail with a note that reads, "Meet me at my place, Friday, 3:00 P.M." You could also invite him to meet you at the train station for an extra bit of mystery. His mind will start to race and he will begin to imagine erotic things. You are creating the ultimate storybook seduction for him, and you must pay attention to detail. Pack your bag thoughtfully. Plan your dress to be gorgeous, yet simple and comfortable. Use medium grays, and choose something that will either show your cleavage or legs, but not both. Choose something that will travel well and that is versatile. Keep items to a minimum. A particularly arresting outfit is a thick, stylish, gray, coat-style dress. Underneath this dress wear a slippery black satin slip and high heels. Choose makeup that is simple and fresh, but choose a high impact lipstick, such as a raspberry or fire engine red. Nothing goes better with the old fashioned grays than a 1940s diva lipstick. On this trip, you are a lady of the highest quality. You shall never be caught without your lipstick.

Pulse Point Oil

YELLOW ROSE

Combine ten drops rose oil with three drops melon and one drop gardenia. Add equal amounts jojoba oil if using pure essential oils. This is a lovely and ladylike fragrance that you may wish to use every morning as you throw on a vintage cardigan with pearl buttons. You should dot a cotton ball with this oil, seal it in plastic wrap, poke a few holes with a pin, and place it in your travel bag. You will not need to apply your perfume again; your clothes will bear a light air of the scent, which will never overpower.

How to Serve the Poem

Compose your own poem, or use the one at the beginning of the chapter. Write the poem on a small note card. Make it something simple and elegant. Attach the note to a small bunch of roses (five or six yellow roses with some loose pink petals mixed in among the flowers and leaves). Remove all of the thorns from the stems. Get a long strand of raffia and start wrapping at the bottom of the bouquet. Wrap tightly and stop midway to secure the note. Get one more rose for your hair. Make sure it's a small one, and cut most of the stem off of it. Use thin wire to wrap the stem to the top of a large bobby pin. Only a fresh rose will work for this effect, and the flower will create an aura of scent around you. Give the bouquet to him on the train or at the train station. He can leave the flowers on the train when you depart but he will want to keep the note with him always. This is the first time that you are saying, "I love you," and there is no doubt that he will say it back. You are his fantasy.

Menu:

CUCUMBER SANDWICHES AND LEMON CREAM SODAS OR LEMON SODAS (NONALCOHOLIC)

This menu is light and will not weigh heavily on your stomachs, as many people suffer some degree of motion sickness when they travel. Cucumbers are actually very calming to the body, as is lemon soda. Since this seduction is all about the interaction between the two of you, there is no need to involve a complex menu. He already knows that you know what's best for every occasion, and he will accept that you know what's best for this one. If you are a bit hungry later on in the trip, take advantage of the great romance of the dining car. Hopefully, it will have a whimsical 1920's feel to its design. Enjoy a light snack together, listening to the soft clickety-clack of the train and imagine simpler days when simply finding each other was enough. Look at each other and feel your connection.

Activity

TRAIN RIDE

He will arrive at your place on time and with his bag. You will both be anxiously anticipating the ride, as untold sensual things will happen. Make yourself comfortable in your car and make sure you are underway before you begin anything physical. He will be surprised and pleased if you are not wearing any panties under your skirt or dress. Enjoy your drinks and the cucumber sandwiches. Have all the fun that you desire. Cover him in rose petals and make love in them. Take some of them to the hotel with you.

The Morning After
WAKE AND DINE IN ANOTHER CITY

Spend the next day touring around in the new exciting locale, drink coffee, and taste eggs and pastries at a tiny café; dine at an unusual restaurant, and walk through whimsical stores and promenades. Buy a small token to remind you of this day, and make sure that you both take the time to repeat the most important thing—that you love each other.

RECIPES

Cucumber Sandwiches

These are very tasty and very cute. The combination of the drink and these tiny sandwiches will really make you feel as if you are already in another land.

Eight slices white bread, crusts trimmed
Butter
½ of a medium-width cucumber, peeled and sliced paper-thin.

Use a rolling pin to flatten the slices of the bread. Do not squish them, but make them significantly thinner. Spread a thin layer of butter on each slice of bread, arrange slices of cucumber, and press the sandwiches together. Use a heart-, flower-, or circle-shaped cookie cutter to cut the sandwiches. Pack in plastic and place in a wicker basket.

Lemon Cream Sodas or Lemon Sodas (nonalcoholic)

Pack the following items in small basket:
2 cans lemon soda
One small bottle of creamy vanilla liqueur (available in fine liquor stores)
Two small glasses

When on the train, find ice to chill the liqueur and the soda. Place one ice cube in each glass, pour one ounce of the liqueur, and fill with lemon soda. If you prefer not to use the liqueur, simply leave it out.

You Make Me Want You

Poem
"Last Night"

Activity
A Sumptuous Meal

Pulse Point Oil
Cherry

Color Scheme
Red

Menu
Lobster Dinner, Pink Champagne or
Pink Cherry Lemonade, and
Chocolate-Covered Strawberries

The Morning After
Your Favorite Diner

Last Night

During the day I could keep my mind on other things
but at night I could only see your face.
Each line, each feature stayed with me.
I saw you in a shadow as I lay in bed.
Your wonderful eyes stared urgently into mine and your lips,
soft and full, opened sensually and invited me to come to you.
I hurried to fall asleep knowing that I could only touch you in dreams.
Sleep didn't come easily.
I fought to feel your kisses but your illusion
only hovered over me, reaching to me.
I tried to touch you but couldn't.
I squeezed my eyes shut and asked you to pull me into the shadows with you.
I want you to come closer until your lips touch
my ear and hear you whisper that you want me.
I finally drifted to sleep and you moved over me.
The heat in your eyes burned through me and
I lay still so I could feel you without thinking of my own movements.
Then your body came down onto me,
My thigh moved up the outside of your leg, and your mouth teased closer to mine.
I felt your breath cooling my hot forehead.
Your eyes looked into mine and they became darker, and the black deeper.
So beautiful that I couldn't see anything else.
I was there, wanting, for your every desire.
Closer, and they grew impatient.
Then you kissed me hard and held me tighter until I felt every inch of you pressing,
and I answered your eyes,
"I want you, too," in an urgent whisper.

*T*onight you are doing all that you need to do to show him that now he must worship you. You are giving him a clear message. With this poem and this meal he will know that tomorrow he must reciprocate, and for every day thereafter. Tonight is his total indulgence, so being bashful isn't on the menu.

Setting the Scene

For this evening's rose ritual, you will need to buy two dozen roses. Red is best, but you can use whatever is available. Leave a trail of rose petals from the front door to the table, and on the bed. Scatter some petals among the sheets and pillows so that you will literally be languishing in them. Wear your favorite dress. It need not be red, but it must be your favorite. This evening should begin just after sunset. Proceed to the dinner table where the chilled pink champagne or pink cherry lemonade will be waiting. Use your bare hands to dip succulent chunks of lobster into the butter sauce and feed each other. Make sure to get all buttery and cute with the food. Don't worry about making a mess, you can lick each other's fingers.

Make sure you thoroughly enjoy sinking into the rose petals in your bed and moving around in them. I encourage you to use old sheets when you do this. Rose petals stain, and those stains do not come out. You may want to remove the petals before falling asleep, as you probably do not want to wake up with large pink blotches all over you.

Before the date is to begin, give yourself an hour to prepare, and spend twenty minutes of that hour in a hot, cherry bubble bath. Keep a bottle of this fabulous soap handy for when you need a quick pick-me-up.

Cherry Bubble Bath

8 oz unscented, good quality bubble bath
1 tbsp corn syrup
¼ cup glycerin
2 tsp cherry essential oil
6 drops red food coloring

Mix glycerin, soap, and corn syrup, stirring gently. Add the oils and food coloring. Stir and pour into any decorative bottle and keep by the bathtub. When starting the water for the tub, run 3 tablespoons of this soap under the water. Have the water run fairly hot. Keep the bottle nearby so you can add more later. Sip strawberry champagne in the tub and nibble some chocolate-covered strawberries.

Pulse Point Oil
CHERRY

Use the cherry oil very sparingly, or you will smell like a fruit salad. You only want to smell just a little bit sweeter. Dot your wrists with just a tiny bit. Try using the cherry under your usual signature scent for an exciting change. Any woody or floral scent will be brightened instantly. Dot a tiny bit onto the lightbulb of the bedside lamp, and add just one drop to the wax of a lit candle.

How to Serve the Poem

Compose your own poem, or use the one at the beginning of the chapter. Leave this poem on a card on a bed pillow with a rose petal on the inside, a pink lipstick imprint, and a drop of your usual perfume. Apply the perfume to the back of the card so that it will not make a stain.

Menu
LOBSTER DINNER, PINK CHAMPAGNE OR PINK CHERRY LEMONADE, AND CHOCOLATE-COVERED STRAWBERRIES

This evening, the meal is your activity. Do not complicate things by arranging any other activity. You want to concentrate on each other's bodies tonight. Use this night as your playground. Do whatever your heart and body wants to. Eat and drink and kiss as much as you want to. You obviously want this man, and the preparation of live Maine lobster should only be done for the special person in your life.

Activity
A SUMPTUOUS MEAL

You trust this individual and you know you can be totally at ease with him. Make him feel comfortable as well. You may bring the meal with you into bed if you want, and he'll use your belly as a serving dish. The belly button makes a cute butter dish, and you can certainly eat the lobster off of his abs or chest and lick the butter from the small hollow at the base of his neck. It is messier, but you can always shower and change the sheets later. You can eat on the floor, outside on the grass, or while naked on a Persian rug. Start soft blues in the background and have a pot of coffee ready to go for after dinner. Make sure that you indulge in every action that you most intimately desire. By now, you should know that he will respect you in the morning.

The Morning After

YOUR FAVORITE DINER

Wake up together, shower together, help each other dress, and make the bed together. Bring a rose to breakfast at your absolute favorite place. Cost should be no issue. The perfect evening can only be followed by the perfect morning. Eat slowly, sip coffee indulgently, play with the rose's petals and smell its fragrance. Know that you are the most beautiful woman he has ever been with. Share every feeling and afterthought with him, the man you love.

RECIPES

Lobster with Butter Sauce

This meal is complete and will take some preparation time, but unlike the other seductions where you have the luxury of dining out and retreating to your home afterward, this evening your home is the retreat. You will play with this meal, and the lobster will seduce the both of you. Most people believe that lobster is difficult to prepare. This couldn't be further from the truth. All that is required of you is to steam it and them remove it from its shell. The butter sauce is well flavored and easy to make, as are the chocolate-covered strawberries. This meal is very impressive, but is deceptively simple to prepare. It will impress your date tremendously, and that is why you will be preparing the entire meal yourself.

Buy two live lobsters, about one pound each.

Some grocery stores with a good seafood department will steam lobsters and other shellfish for you. Take advantage of this luxury if you can. Otherwise use the following instructions.

Plunge the lobsters, headfirst, into a large pot of boiling, salted water. Cover and boil ten to twelve minutes. Remove as soon as the lobsters are bright red. Remove the lobster with tongs and place on its back. Slit the undershell lengthwise with a sharp knife or scissors. Remove and discard the dark vein, the sack near the head, all of the organs and all the spongy tissue. Remove the tail and clean out the cavity on the top. Replace the top flap of meat and put the tail back into the shell. Use a nutcracker or lobster cracker for cracking the claws, trying to save the top part of the claw to place the meat back into and place on a large, flat plate, right-side-up. Reheat for 1 minute in the microwave right before serving and garnish with parsley and a lemon wedge.

Butter Sauce

½ tsp garlic juice
¼ cup butter
1 tsp lemon juice
Dash of Tabasco
Salt and pepper to taste

Mix all the ingredients in a bowl and microwave in twenty-second bursts until hot and completely melted. Stir after twenty seconds. Butter warmers are little metal dish contraptions with a candle beneath. These will keep the butter melted throughout the meal. Taste the butter before serving; it may need more salt, pepper, or Tabasco.

Steamed Asparagus

Buy one bunch of asparagus from the market, remove ten stalks, and wash them. Put the rest in the refrigerator for your later consumption. Break the ends off where they break naturally and remove the bottom scales with a vegetable peeler. Place on a plate with a bit of water on the bottom and cover with plastic wrap. Microwave on high for about four minutes until tender. Arrange three or four stalks on each of the plates and sprinkle with a bit of salt.

Chocolate Covered Strawberries

12 large, ripe strawberries
4 oz milk chocolate

Melt the chocolate in a double boiler until smooth. Do not heat the chocolate too quickly or it will burn. Dip the strawberries quickly and place on a sheet of wax paper. Let cool and harden at room temperature for at least one and a half hours. Do not chill in the refrigerator or they will have moisture on them later. These are only delicious on the first day, so do not attempt to make these beforehand.

Pink Champagne

In a chilled tulip glass combine:
½ oz grenadine
1 drop red food coloring

Fill with chilled champagne. Drop a raspberry or a few currants in.

If you wish, you can lightly rub a lemon wedge around the rim of the glass and then dip it in powdered sugar, and shake off the excess.

Pink Cherry Lemonade

In a large glass combine:
Ice
1 oz cherry syrup (for shaved ice or Italian sodas)

Fill with pink lemonade. Garnish with maraschino cherries.

The Revealing Seduction

Poem
"My Fantasy"

Activity
Moonlight Walk

Pulse Point Oil
Vanilla

Color Scheme
Black as the Night

Menu
Damiana Bread Dip,
Crab Stuffed Snow Peas, and
Chilled Champagne or
Green Fantasia Cocktail (nonalcoholic)

The Morning After
Mexican Coffee

My Fantasy

I follow your silvery shadow in the moonlight.

A whiteness that glows in the coldness of this night.

The hot, silky skin of your nakedness steaming.

The shape of your muscles awakens my needing.

You hear me and turn, your eyes hold me stricken.

And when you walk toward me the fog seems to thicken.

I grope through the mist, feel you reaching to find me.

I turn at a sound and then feel you behind me.

Your hands reach around me and heat up my skin.

You kiss me, my lover, push into me then.

You hold my waist, draw back, then push again harder.

The fog, our thick blanket, drifts off and then farther.

Then there's only us, one shining shadow in the moonlight.

A whiteness that glows in the warmth of this night.

*T*onight you will be serving a Mexican appetizer and champagne, then going for a seductive moonlit walk. If you are hungry after walking, head to a Mexican restaurant and have a big meal. Afterwards, come back to your place and sip champagne and reminisce, or put on some salsa music and dance. If you really want to impress your date, invest in two or three salsa lessons just to teach you how to move your hips. Above all, be yourself, do not be afraid to twirl and use your curves to their best advantage with your salsa moves.

Setting the Scene

Turn all the lights off for the evening, using only candlelight to see. A cute trick is to paint glow-in-the-dark stars on the ceiling directly above your bed, maybe in the constellation of your or his birth sign. Start off with about twenty identical, thin, black candles grouped together on one table and blow one out every twenty minutes or so. Eventually have only one or two candles. Mix in a few scented candles, not too many though, as you don't want a synthetic, fruity smell to dominate. One fruity candle and one woody scented candle added to the mix will be fine.

A perfect flower for this evening is either a bunch of dark purple pansies or purple-black roses. The roses may be hard to find, but are very beautiful if you succeed. The purple easily complements black and is usually mistaken for black in a home environment. There are also sunflowers with purple stems and leaves, and flowers that are deep reddish-orange. These are fantastic if you can find them, last a long time, and do not lend an overpowering scent. Arrange one or two candles of the same dark purple near the vase.

Get a small spotlight and rig it as an up-light in front of a large plant to cast shadows against the wall. Make sure that the lamp is hidden and safely positioned.

Pulse Point Oil

VANILLA

Prepare a batch of vanilla perfume (recipes follows), then dab the perfume on your pulse points and add a drop to the lightbulb in the bathroom. Use a tiny dab the following morning if the scent has dissipated by then. The orange oil makes this perfume very unique, and the addition of the sandalwood makes it more sexual and less musky in nature.

Vanilla Perfume

1 tbsp vanilla essential oil
½ tsp sandalwood oil

3 drops orange oil

1 tbsp glycerin

Add a few drops of water

Keep in a tiny bottle by the bed and dab very sparingly on pulse points just before the date. You can also put a drop or two on a lightbulb to slowly disperse the fragrance.

Menu

Damiana Bread Dip, Crab Stuffed Snow Peas, and Chilled Champagne or Green Fantasia Cocktail (nonalcoholic)

Damiana is a Mexican spice, and is an ethnic aphrodisiac. It does not have a strong flavor and is a pleasant additive to any dip for bread. Spicy food, in general, has aphrodisiac qualities, as it can slightly increase blood pressure and make your face glow warm. He will be attracted to that glow like a moth to a flame.

Activity

Moonlight Walk

If it is warm outside, take a moonlit walk and kiss under a tree. Having a glass of champagne before you go will warm you. Memorize a poem beforehand, and whisper it to him in the dark. Bring a light blanket with you so you can sit down and look up at the stars. Sitting quietly under the tree of a neighbor will feel scandalous and may make you want to try some other risky behavior. Do this only if your neighborhood is safe and quiet. If you have access to a body of water, you may wish to skinny dip. Of course, wearing a trench coat with nothing on underneath is always a fantastic surprise for a date. You may otherwise want to have on something little and silky.

Have a soft blanket waiting on the sofa so when you get back you can cuddle up. Tickle the bottoms of his bare feet with your own.

The Morning After

Mexican Coffee

Enjoy Mexican coffee the next morning. It will flood you both with feelings of last night and may inspire some morning action as well.

RECIPES

Damiana Bread Dip

Combine a few droppers full of Damiana tincture to a mixture of olive oil, fresh garlic, and balsamic vinegar.

Slice a French baguette thinly and diagonally and serve with the dip. Use the dip sparingly and feed each other. Alternate sips of champagne or green fantasia cocktail with the appetizer.

Crab Stuffed Snow Peas

2 dozen fresh snow peas or sugar snap peas (large)
1 small can crab meat (fresh lump crabmeat from a fish market)
2 tbsp mayonnaise
1 tbsp finely chopped chives
salt and pepper to taste

Wash the peas and dry. Carefully slice the seam edge with a sharp knife. Remember to cut away from your hand and body. Carefully insert the knife into the pea and expand the opening a bit. Pick over the crab to remove any bits of shell or cartilage, but do not wash the crab, as it will take away the flavor.

In a small bowl combine remaining ingredients and mix with a fork. Season to taste and add a bit more mayonnaise if necessary. Spoon the mixture into an icing bag with a round nozzle. Inset nozzle into each pea pod and slowly squeeze in the filling. Only a little filling is necessary, as it is very flavorful.

Arrange pea pods like petals of a flower on a small, round platter with a slice or two of lemon to drizzle right before serving.

Champagne

Chill the champagne well ahead of time in the refrigerator and serve in tall champagne flutes. Remember to point the bottle away from you when uncorking. Choosing champagne for your meal is easy if you follow these very simple steps:

• Ask yourself, "How much would I like to spend?" Do not go over that amount. You can get a perfectly good champagne for less than twenty dollars.

- Decide whether you like sweet or dry wines.
- Call someone you trust to be knowledgeable in that area, or go to a liquor store in or near an expensive neighborhood, and tell them what you are looking for and what you will be serving it with. Listen to their recommendations, but decide for yourself in the end. Go ahead and be adventurous—if you don't like your choice, you'll just know more the next time.
- Never buy Dom Perignon if you are not too fond of champagne. You will only end up angry with yourself for having wasted the money.
- If you wish to add some flare to the champagne, soak a sugar cube in a few drops of bitters, and place it and a strawberry in the bottom of the glass. This is known as a champagne cocktail.

Green Fantasia Cocktail
In a large, chilled glass combine:
Ice
1 oz orange juice
1 oz grenadine

Fill most of the way with pineapple juice. Top with a splash of green syrup (shaved ice syrups work nicely for colorful cocktails).

Mexican Coffee
¼ –½ oz tequila
½ oz Kahlua
Fresh, hot coffee

Pour liquors into coffee mug and add hot, fresh coffee. If using a glass mug, put a metal spoon in it first to disperse the heat of the coffee, or the mug may break. Garnish with whipped cream and a sprinkle of cinnamon and a cinnamon stick.

If you prefer a coffee with a strong cinnamon flavor, replace the tequila with ½ oz. Goldschlager. Goldschlager is very hot cinnamon schnapps, and has little pieces of gold floating in it. Gold is edible and this also adds a wonderful glimmer to the drink. Strain out a few of the gold pieces and top the whip cream with them right before serving. Gold dust is available from fine bakeries for this purpose as well.

For a nonalcoholic coffee, top plain coffee with whipped cream, a sprinkling of cinnamon, and white confectioner's sugar.

Waves of Seduction

Poem
"Surrender Your Body to Me"

Activity
Sharing Your Fantasies

Pulse Point Oil
Sweet Springtime Pillow Mist

Color Scheme
Sea Green and Blue

Menu
Black Forest Cheesecake and
Chocolate Martini or
Molasses Milkshake

The Morning After
French Pastries and Tea

Surrender Your Body to Me

Stranded in the oceans of you, you move me with a swell.

Liquid, my body moves with you, controlled by you.

My will has deserted me and so you keep me adrift.

It is a dark-night sea, but warm, and

we are alone on the horizon.

Your watery hands wash over my skin as you press my back into the sand.

I can feel all your strength.

You rush into the shore, rush into me.

Your body asks me to set myself free and wild with the current.

It's raining.

You loosen your grip from my arms and I run and I tease you to claim me.

My nightdress is transparent.

It clings to my wet body and restricts my movement.

It catches at my legs.

You seize me and pull me down on the sand.

Rain falls on our bodies, cooling.

The dress washes away with the tide, and

I let go.

This seduction creates an atmosphere of easy sensuality. The date is to take place in the early evening as the sun is setting, so it is best for a Saturday when the day is all your own. Go to the beach (a secluded one is best) or another body of water. Be sure that both of you walk around barefoot and bury each other's feet in the sand. Play footsie. Feel the sand and its roughness on your skin, on your arms, legs, and hands. It is a great sensation.

Setting the Scene

Arrange items of fancy around your dining and sofa area in an ocean motif. On your television, play a video of underwater scenes. You can buy a video like this at a bookstore that carries educational videos such as National Geographic or Jacques Cousteau's documentaries. You can play a CD of ocean sounds quietly in the background with the television muted, use a few pretty seashells on the table, or, if you have a big enough shell, you can place a candle in it.

Before the date begins you will be enjoying a sexy watery experience (a fantastic bath) that is intended just for you. Do this about an hour and a half before. This soak will invigorate you, fill you with sexual energy, and give you a sense of peaceful calm. Buy large rock salt for the tub, and place it in a large, wide shell. Draw a warm bath. Do not make the water too hot, or the fragrance oils will take on a very pungent nature. Also, a hot bath would make you drowsy. Add a few drops of anise or pine essential oil to the bath water. These strong fragrances will stimulate your senses and keep you feeling very alive throughout the evening. Make sure you use these oils sparingly; you do not want them to overpower. Light two pale green or blue candles and place them at the two corners of the tub by your feet. Enjoy the bath for about fifteen minutes. Feel the salts revitalize you and just relax. Absorb the peace and close your eyes, thinking of the soft candlelight. Ease yourself out of the water and smooth a light sesame oil over your skin. Allow yourself five or so minutes to allow your skin to air dry and absorb the silky oil. It will make your skin satiny but will not leave a residue.

Select the lingerie that you would like to wear under your clothing, and put it on slowly, enjoying how well it fits you. Hang the clothing on a decorative hook on your closet door, placed there for this purpose, and continue arranging your environment as you so desire. Place a small bowl of pretty pieces of beach glass by your bedside or on a windowsill to catch late evening sunrays.

You may wish to glue a small shell to a bobby pin for securing your hair, or use store-bought, body-jewelry glue to secure a little starfish or sand dollar shell to your throat or in your belly button, depending on what you are wearing. I had a tiny starfish gold-plated for this purpose.

You can glue it to your chest above your cleavage to attract attention there, or glue it to your temple or upper arm. A pearl makes a great belly button accessory and small half-pearls (available in bead- and jewelry-making stores) are great for glued-on choker necklaces and upper-arm bracelets.

Pulse Point Oil
SWEET SPRINGTIME PILLOW MIST
This perfect pillow mist can be made months ahead of time and still smell delicious. It is a great idea always to have some of this by your bed. You'll want to use it often— even when you're alone.

30 drops strawberry fragrance oil
5 drops each tangerine and orange
3 drops lemon
4 drops rose
1 drop vanilla
2 tbsp vodka
1 ½ tsp vegetable glycerin

Mix all oils together in a small atomizer bottle. Add vodka and glycerin. Cap and shake. Let sit overnight to marry essences. Give your pillows, sheets, and lampshade a light dusting about ten minutes before sinking into the bed (whether alone or not). You will have the nicest dreams.

How to Serve the Poem
Compose your own poem, or use the one at the beginning of the chapter. Write the poem on an old piece of paper, roll it up, and insert it into the end of a small, corked jar. Add a small handful of sand to it before corking and lay it next to his place setting.

Menu
BLACK FOREST CHEESECAKE AND CHOCOLATE MARTINI OR MOLASSES MILKSHAKE
Walk to a beachfront café to eat a light lunch. Try some freshly steamed crab legs or oysters. Imitation crab is also a tasty alternative when served in a salad. Relax and savor the time that you can just be with each other without overdoing the words. There are many treats in store

for both of you tonight. When you arrive back at your place, take time to properly enjoy the drinks and cheesecake, and definitely try the spun-sugar pastries.

Activity
SHARING YOUR FANTASIES
You both may not be used to openly sharing your fantasies, and you may want to keep the really questionable stuff to yourself, but definitely try it. In order to feel more comfortable with what you are sharing, write it down before the date starts. Make a little story out of it. You are the star of this story. Just start writing, and I promise you that a great fantasy will emerge. Maybe you would like to make love on an airplane, or underwater. Perhaps you would like to fool around in a canoe while paddling through primitive, crocodile-infested waters. On a simpler note, you could fantasize about taking a bath in champagne while being fed small chocolates. Whatever you want, share it. You may get it. Encourage your date to open up about his deepest fantasies. Tell each other your fantasies over dim light. Wouldn't it be great if his fantasy was to have you as his dessert? If so, adorn your nipples with these candy pastries after the meal. They adhere well when moistened with your tongue and they are really very tasty. Sip the chocolate martinis or molasses shake while enjoying the cake. This should put the both of you into a very relaxed mood. Get creative and be honest.

The Morning After
FRENCH PASTRIES AND TEA
Purchase brioche or another delicious French pastry from a good local bakery. Serve a pastry on a delicate little saucer with a fresh rose petal. Serve hot tea and use a small teapot and tiny teacups for each of you. Men enjoy the fantasy of antique cups and saucers as much as women. It brings you back to a more innocent age and makes those deep glances across the table very meaningful, indeed.

RECIPES

Black Forest Cheesecake

1 ½ cups chocolate cookie crumbs

3 tbsp margarine

2 8-oz packages cream cheese, softened

1 14-oz can chocolate-flavored, condensed milk

3 eggs

3 tbsp corn starch

1 tsp almond extract

1 21-oz can cherry pie filling

Preheat oven to 300° F. Combine crumbs and margarine, and press firmly over the bottom of a nine-inch springform pan. In a large bowl, beat the cream cheese until fluffy. Gradually beat in condensed milk until smooth. Add eggs, cornstarch, and almond extract, and mix well.

Pour into prepared pan. Bake about 35 minutes until a knife inserted into the center comes out clean. Cool, then chill. Top with the pie filling before serving. Use aerosol whip cream to make a thin border around the top of the cake and stick the toffee pastries in it. Put two together to make a neat ball-like shape, and place it securely in the cream.

Chocolate Martini

These are truly the greatest martinis. Make chocolate-decorated cocktail glasses ahead of time and keep in the refrigerator until ready to use.

Melt a small amount of milk chocolate chips in the microwave at 30-second bursts. Drizzle chocolate inside the glasses, making stripes in one direction. Let cool 10 minutes. Repeat the process in the other direction, creating a crisscross pattern, using white chocolate if you wish. Let cool. Coat the rims of the glasses by running them through a small amount of melted chocolate in a dish. Let cool. You may like to keep a couple of these prepared glasses in your pantry. For storing, lightly cover the chocolate-coated areas with plastic wrap.

In a metal mixing cup combine:

Ice

1 oz White Crème de Cocoa

1 oz brown creme de cocoa

2 oz vodka

2 oz cream (use milk for a lighter, slightly less scrumptious drink)

Shake and strain into the two chilled cocktail glasses. Use the chocolate-rimmed glasses, or drop a Hershey's kiss into each glass, or top each drink with a bit of whipped cream and sprinkle on chocolate shavings (you can easily make chocolate shavings by using a vegetable peeler on a bar of chocolate). Use less vodka and more cream if the taste is too strong.

Molasses Shake

Combine in a blender:

1 tsp molasses

8 oz cold milk

A small handful of ice

Blend until pureed, and top the milkshake with whipped cream and caramel sauce. Serve with the cheesecake.

Spun Sugar Pastries

These sweet little things are absolutely priceless. They keep for a while between sheets of wax paper while stored in a cool, dry place, but they are best made no earlier than the day before. They can also be made out of chocolate using the same method, but those melt faster and aren't quite as much fun to eat. Do not freeze or refrigerate as they will collect moisture and lose their crisp texture. Your playfulness will never be forgotten.

Make a small, wide cone out of wax paper by cutting to the middle of a circle of wax paper and overlapping slightly. Tape securely. Make four or five.

Dissolve one-fourth cup white sugar in one-fourth cup boiling water. Microwave on high power for three to four minutes until syrup is golden. Coat the back of two wooden spoons with the sugar. Touch and draw the spoons apart to form fine strands. Hold the spoons over the wax paper cones one at a time and drop the mixture in to form a crisscross pattern.

If the sugar becomes too thick, microwave on high in 20 second bursts until softened. When done with each pastry, use a knife to cut off the excess from the base of the shape while it is still fairly soft. Let sit until cool, and put in a cool, dry place until ready to use. Be very careful when removing them from the paper, as they sometimes break. It is for this reason that I prefer to make eight or so at a time just in case.

The Confident Seduction

Poem
"Maybe You Should Stay the Night"

Activity
Sensual Massage

Pulse Point Oil
Lemon Verbena

Color Scheme
Yellow and Orange

Menu
Baked Oysters and
Perfect Martinis or
Virgin Bliss

The Morning After
Cheese and Mushroom Omelette

Maybe You Should Stay the Night

I trace the pale blue line with my eyes and my fingers.
Very light, barely noticeable.
A ghost shadow on your skin.
I follow it up your ankle and calf, almost losing it in your tan.
I grow nervous, as this would be our first time if
I let my hand wander too far and for too long.
I look away for a moment to touch you without seeing.
I feel your electricity running from your skin into my fingertips,
into my blood,
searching for its mate.
I look again.
You're leaning against large pillows and
rumpled linen sheets and
I know you can catch the whisper of the perfume I wore just for you.
I think for a moment about waiting as I have night after night.
Again I lay with you,
hating and praising myself for my purity.
But here you are; naked, warm, and
looking into me with eyes that I haven't seen on other nights.
I notice the same faint blue line on your neck.
I lean in to give it a soft kiss, and
then harder and I feel you lean your head back and I think.
What if this time I don't say no?

*W*hen you are the tiger who has spotted your prey, this is how you will pounce. You will get the physical attention you are looking for with this poem, so you should be ready for it, mentally and physically. This is a great poem for the evening that you will be sharing as massage is mentioned in the poem and is also to be performed. Your erotic intentions cannot and will not be mistaken.

Begin the date late on a Saturday afternoon and have him take you to dinner at a place where you can languish over expensive, wonderfully presented entrees. Make sure you eat enough so that you will not be starving later in the evening, as a menu of cocktails and oysters is not going to be very filling. You want to seduce your date, not show him how domestic you are.

Setting the Scene

To set the mood, arrange a centerpiece of small yellow flowers on your table, surrounding the vase with small votive candles.

Start some soft music—jazz is always easy to listen to in the background, especially if you're not paying attention. It becomes as natural and unnoticeable as the wallpaper. Sit close together at the table so that you will be able to feed each other, and so your date will be able to catch your scent. This is a perfect meal to enjoy outside; so, if you have a patio or small balcony, you should set up the table there. Citronella candles are an easy solution to any pest problems.

Ask your date questions about himself. If you already know each other well, take this time to listen deeply to anything he has to say. Just listen for a while, and he will feel like he knows you even better.

You should have the blankets laid out in a part of your home where there is a large space on the floor. It will seem as though there is nothing else in the room except the two of you. Make sure the temperature in the room is not cold. Increase the heat by a few degrees if necessary.

The massage should be to candlelight and soft, slow music. Avoid sounds that are too soothing as your date may fall asleep. Use music with a gentle beat or with a twang such as a sitar. Arrange a pretty blanket on the floor and place soft pillows and towels underneath for comfort and contours, and to absorb some of the oil. Use warm orange colors to make your date feel warm all over. Encourage him to massage you as well. The oil should be easily accessible in a small bowl for dipping your fingers right into. Place the bowl by a candle to catch the light. You may try warming the oil in the microwave for twenty seconds right before use. Test for temperature first to make sure it is not too hot.

You can burn incense—one orange and one vanilla make a wonderful combination. Keep the incense in a room away from where you'll be spending the evening. It should only be a light background scent to be barely detected. If burning incense does not interest you, you can place a drop or two of an essential oil onto either the flowers in the vase or into a small bowl into which you have put a small pile of the flower petals. Carnation is the perfect oil for this as it is also used in the massage oil and provides a clean and fresh background scent.

Pulse Point Oil
LEMON VERBENA
The lemon verbena oil should only be dabbed onto the main pulse points (right behind the ear lobes, on the center of the wrist, in the crook of the elbow, and right behind the knee), and used in very small amounts. Behind the knee is always a good place to use perfumes as well, as the scent travels upward as you move and your body grows warmer. Lemon verbena is also a very potent aroma, and you do not want it to overpower. Remember that the scent of the massage oil will be strong on both of you as well, so the lemon verbena may only linger at dinner. If the oil is pure, dilute it with a third of the volume of jojoba oil, as pure aromatherapy oils are not meant to be worn directly on the skin unless they are adequately diluted.

Men greatly enjoy this fragrance as well. It is fresh and clean and has a delightful pungency, which is neither masculine nor feminine, and does not overpower. Try placing a cotton ball that has been dipped with the oil into his tie drawer.

How to Serve the Poem
Compose your own poem, or use the one at the beginning of the chapter. Write the poem on an antique-looking piece of paper and leave it by the vase with your favorite antique fountain pen on top of it. Allow him to read it just before beginning massage.

Menu
BAKED OYSTERS AND PERFECT MARTINIS OR VIRGIN BLISS
Take as much time as you desire to enjoy your oysters—they are a very sensual food. They have an interesting texture and taste that teases the tongue. This particular dish is smooth, salty, and spicy, while being tangy and refreshing. Try to notice the flavor of the martini as it mixes with that of the oysters. Pay attention to your tongue, and how it reacts. Feel the oysters slip down your throat and enjoy the spicy and lemony afterglow.

Activity

SENSUAL MASSAGE

Start by mixing your own perfect blend of massage oil:

¼ tsp anisette essential oil

½ tsp each of cucumber, geranium, narcissus, and rose essential oils

½ tsp vitamin E oil

8 oz grape seed oil

Pour grape seed oil in a plastic bottle that will seal tightly. Add the remaining ingredients and shake to blend. Let the oil sit overnight to marry the scents. Pour it into a pretty glass bottle. Keep it in the refrigerator if you would like to try the oil on your partner ice cold. Or store it in a cupboard and microwave it for twenty seconds in a small, pretty bowl right before using.

Begin by having your date get comfortable while you do the same. Either have him strip down to his underwear, or just remove his top. Do not go naked just yet, unless you want to get him nervous. The best way for him to enjoy this massage is to be fully at ease. You should wear whatever you feel is appropriate. A satiny robe with nothing underneath is usually the best way to feel comfortable and free up your movements.

Warm the oil in the microwave and light a few large candles. The larger the candle, the more sensual the environment. At first it may seem too dark with only the few candles. Don't worry, your eyes will adjust and before long it may seem too bright. Place a small pillow on the blankets for him to rest his head on and have him lie face down on the blankets. Sit on the blankets next to him. Dip your fingers into the warmed oil and delicately swirl it on his lower back, adding more until you have enough oil to get messy with. Use pressure and make smooth circles with your fingertips in the middle of the lower back. Concentrate efforts near the spine. Continue the same motion a little higher, also near the spine. Always make circular motions.

The lower back is almost always the most sore, so massage that area for about five minutes before continuing up the spine even further. Add more oil if necessary, and work up the center of the shoulder blades. Stop and start again at the lower back, except this time use gentle up and down strokes with your whole hand while working on his sides. Continue upward until you reach the shoulder blades again. Add more oil if necessary and start working on the upper back. Start at the top of the neck using circular pressure with your fingers. Continue down the neck until you reach the base of the neck. Remain there for a few minutes, with increased pressure for much stress is harbored in that region. Use the thumbs to work out any spots that feel tense. Work out toward the shoulders and then massage the whole shoulder with your hands.

At this point, have him get more comfortable. He may feel that he wishes to remove his pants or underwear now. Seat yourself on his buttocks and continue the shoulder massage. Use good pressure and work slowly now. Start moving down the arms until you get to the hands and ask your date to turn over. He should be very at ease by now, and this should be a welcome advancement. Massage his hands, one at a time, and give attention to the fingers, which are very sensitive touch receptors. Glide your hands up to his shoulders and encourage him to begin massaging your legs.

Now he is completely relaxed and is very comfortable with you and how you treat him. Continue the massage and trade places if you wish.

The Morning After
Cheese and Mushroom Omelette

You may very well wish to share coffee and pastry at a favorite café the next morning, but you may also wish to whip up an omelette at your place. The omelette is intended for two. Enjoy it with hot, fresh coffee. Light a candle on the breakfast table. There is nothing wrong with burning candles during the day; you may find it very calming.

RECIPES

Baked Oysters

Prepare this dish one hour before the date. This will give you time to clean the kitchen counter and wash dishes. This recipe is easy to make and will also work well with fresh water mussels.

2 dozen freshly opened oysters (Purchase from a reputable vendor and have them shuck the live oysters for you.)
2 slices bacon
½ cup minced shallots
4 tbsp minced celery
dash lemon juice
dash Worcestershire sauce
1 drop Tabasco sauce

Preheat the oven to 400° F. Place two drained, washed oysters each on the deep half of one shell. Arrange filled oyster shells on a thin layer of rock salt in a large baking pan. Cook the bacon in a skillet until crisp. Remove from pan, drain, and crumble. To the bacon fat add the scallions and celery and cook until almost tender (about three minutes). Season with the lemon juice, Worcestershire sauce, and Tabasco. Spoon the mixture onto the oysters in the shells and top with the crumbled bacon. Bake ten minutes.

Arrange on an interesting serving platter to which you have added a few shells from the beach. An absolutely beautiful way to serve these is with a large, real pearl placed on top of several oysters by the edge of the shell (be sure not to eat them). I have taken apart a bracelet for this purpose. The pearls can be used for similar dishes with other shellfish, but obviously oysters are the most appropriate choice. In candlelight, the pearls will give the platter a sensual luster. Place a tiny wedge of lemon atop each oyster.

Perfect Martinis

In a metal mixing cup combine:
Ice
6 oz good gin

Dash of dry Vermouth
Dash of sweet Vermouth

Shake and strain into 2 chilled cocktail glasses.

Virgin Bliss
In a tall, chilled glass combine:
Ice
1 oz coconut milk
1 oz cream
4 oz apricot nectar

Stir and garnish with a halved apricot.

Cheese and Mushroom Omelette
1 small potato
2 tbsp vegetable oil
salt and freshly ground pepper to taste
1 tbsp plus 2 tsp butter
½ cup thinly sliced mushrooms
2 eggs
1 tbsp finely diced gruyere or Swiss cheese
2 tsp finely chopped chives

Peel the potato and cut it into one-fourth inch squares. There should be about one-half cup. Put the cubes into a small amount of cold water to prevent discoloration. Drain the potato and pat dry with paper towel. Heat the oil in a small skillet and add the potato. Sprinkle with salt and pepper. Cook, stirring until the potatoes are cooked on all sides, about ten minutes. Drain well.

Heat one tablespoon of butter in a clean skillet and add the mushrooms. Cook until they give up their liquid and continue cooking until the liquid evaporates.

Beat the eggs in a mixing bowl and add the potato, mushrooms, cheese, chives, salt and pepper. Blend well. Heat two teaspoons of butter in a small omelette pan and add the egg mixture. Cook over relatively high heat, shaking the skillet and stirring, until the omelette is set on the bottom. Invert the omelette onto a hot, round serving dish and serve.

Come Back Soon, My Darling

Poem
"Let's Really Live These Few Moments"

Activity
Miniature Golf

Pulse Point Oil
Floral Plum

Color Scheme
Maroon, the Royal Sorrowful Color

Menu
Candied Edible Flowers and
Chinese Dream Cocktails
or Sunset Sweets

The Morning After
Quiche and Café Latte

Let's Really Live These Few Moments

The train station is at the edge of town.

Stand with me on the platform there, and

pull me to you to kiss my neck when the train goes by.

As the train deafens me and your tongue and lips trace my throat,

I imagine all the trips we could have taken

if you could only stay a while longer.

There's a park hidden by trees where we can go when it's raining and

I can touch all of you in the middle of the day.

We can watch the rain hit our bodies,

moving together on the soaked grass, and

listen to it fall knowing that we are safe here.

Look at me in the sunshine with my face in your hands and

we can name all the colors in each other's eyes, and

you can tell me, promise me, that you'll be back soon.

I'll burn a vigil by our bed. I'll fall asleep to the flame and

tell all my love to it.

Tell me only that you love me, and

if you can't stand with me by the train tracks,

at least promise me that your heart will stay behind.

*I*f you must say good-bye, this is the way to say it. No matter what the circumstance, you not only need to express yourself, but you will need to be expressed to. This seduction inspires a pure experience, passion and truth throughout. This should begin late in the evening, and continue into the wee hours. If you are parting for a while, you should try to just enjoy each other's company and not dwell on or talk about how upset you are over the separation.

Setting the Scene

As soon as you come in from the evening's activity, put on some reed flute music (rainstorm or running stream sounds are also pretty). For extra charm, put a vase of maroon tulips by the head of the bed and pile as many soft, decorative pillows as possible on the bed. Add a drop or two of floral plum oil to the liquid wax of the candles you are using, or dab onto the light-bulb in your bedside lamp.

Pulse Point Oil

FLORAL PLUM

Combine twenty drops of plum fragrance oil with five drops of carnation fragrance oil. Add one teaspoon of almond oil. Let the oil sit overnight to marry the scents. Apply it sparingly to the pulse points.

How to Serve the Poem

Compose your own poem, or use the one at the beginning of the chapter. Prepare this message in your finest penmanship with your favorite writing instrument. Enclose the poem in a small envelope on which you will write, "Open when you miss me." Hand this envelope to him as he leaves. Of course, he will open it right away, and will start to miss you painfully and start counting the days until he can see you again.

Menu

CANDIED EDIBLE FLOWERS AND CHINESE DREAM COCKTAILS OR SUNSET SWEETS (NONALCOHOLIC)

Select flowers such as pansies, zucchini flowers, or small violets. These are very lovely and very safe. I like to use such flowers in salads on a regular basis. Guests always love them. You will find these little delights charming. Pick your own, or purchase them at a florist (make sure they do not have any chemicals sprayed on them).

Activity

MINIATURE GOLF

Have a good time together during a charming dinner, and move on to miniature golf, as it will make you both laugh a little, and remind you to have fun together. You do not have to suffer through the good-bye. As much as possible, maintain physical contact throughout the evening. Give him a hug before you sit down to dinner. Hold onto his arm as you walk from one golf hole to the next. On the way back to your place, kiss him at a red light, and keep your hand lightly resting on his knee as he drives. Shift from the din of the miniature golf to a mellow mood as you reach home.

The Morning After

QUICHE AND CAFÉ LATTE

Prepare the quiche the previous day so that you won't interrupt the peaceful mood of the morning. Wake early and prepare the coffee drinks, and enjoy the early dawn as you watch him sleep. Maybe take a picture of his adorable sleeping face. Give him his breakfast in bed on a wooden tray, and place a tiny vase on the tray and a tiny glass of orange juice garnished with a strawberry (wet the strawberry and coat with sugar first). Feed each other forkfuls of quiche. Sip the lattes together and be peaceful; gaze into each other's eyes, and know that it won't be too long before you see each other again.

RECIPES

Candied Edible Flowers

Wash flowers and let them air dry. Whip one egg white with a fork, and mix with a little water. Use a paintbrush to apply the egg whites to the petals of the flowers. Sprinkle the flowers with white sugar while the egg white is wet. Arrange flowers on wax paper and place on a cookie sheet. Bake at 110° F for twenty minutes. Keep an eye on them. You do not want them to overdry. They will shrivel, but the light baking will make the sugar start to take on a caramel flavor. Arrange.

Chinese Dream Cocktails

1 oz ginger liqueur
½ oz Kahlua
½ oz White Crème de Cocoa
¼ cup milk
1 scoop vanilla ice cream
strawberry sauce
whipped cream
shaved chocolate

Blend these ingredients in a blender until smooth, pour into a large hurricane glass. Add strawberry sauce (an ice cream topping) by pouring down the sides and swirling around edges and sides of the glass. Top with whip cream and shaved chocolate.

Sunset Sweets

In two small glasses combine:
Ice
Fill mostly full with orange juice or orange soda

Top with 1 oz grenadine. Garnish with three cherries.

Café Latte

In a beautiful coffee cup, mix two ounces of very strong coffee or espresso and fill the rest of the way with hot, steamed milk. Top with whipped cream; let the whipped cream melt into the coffee, and sprinkle cinnamon on top.

Quiche

Remember to make this rich, delicious dish the day before.

Frozen pastry for a 9-inch pie crust, defrosted
1 small onion, finely chopped
¾ cup cubed Swiss cheese
¼ cup grated parmesan cheese
4 eggs, beaten
1 cup cream
1 cup nonfat milk
½ tsp nutmeg
dash of salt
¼ tsp pepper
2 cups dried beans of any type

Preheat oven to 375° F. Line a pie plate with the pastry and cover with foil. Cover the foil with dried beans and bake for 20 minutes. These beans will keep the pastry from bubbling or lifting off the pie plate. Remove foil and beans. Set aside. Sauté the onions in a little butter until transparent. Scatter the onions and cheese in the bottom of the piecrust. Combine eggs, cream, milk, and spices, and pour through a sieve into the piecrust. Bake 40 to 45 minutes or until a knife inserted into the center comes out clean.

The Reunion

Poem
"Come Back to Me Now"

Activity
Slow and Sexy Partner Yoga

Pulse Point Oil
Orange Blossom

Color Scheme
Crisp "Daybreak White"

Menu
Dine Out at a French Restaurant,
Then Serve Fresh, Black Caviar,
and Iced Vodka or Balsamic Vinegar
Tincture (nonalcoholic)

The Morning After
Lox with Capers, Hot Coffee

Come Back to Me Now

I only imagine where you are each passing moment and
I am jealous of the people nearby.
For they are near you. They see you, hear you speak,
They watch you move and can breathe in your sexiness.
And I am jealous of the air around you.
It touches your skin and feels you beneath your clothing.
It kisses you without you knowing. It can touch your cheek, your chest,
your stomach, your thigh,
and you cannot turn it away.
Please dream of me where you'll sleep tonight.
Only tonight and return to me tomorrow.
Taste me in your mind before sleep steals you,
knows your deepest thoughts and your urges.
If I could be in your bed only for a sleeping moment, and let my mouth
feel you again.
And if I could be air only for tomorrow so I could breathe into you again.
Then I will be satisfied.
Then I will have you again.

*P*repare this seduction when he is returning from a trip. Make a list of your amorous thoughts while he is away and keep them with you. Reminding yourself of how sexy he is will make you all the more sexually powerful when he walks through the door. You may wish to slip the list into his jacket pocket so that he finds it one day, or you can keep it in your pocketbook to heat you up anytime before a date.

Setting the Scene

First plan to have an early dinner at a tiny, French restaurant. Try Pernod if they have it. It is a strong anisette flavored liquor. The French mix one part Pernod with five parts ice water to produce a clean licorice taste, and a fascinating opalescent milky-blue color. Only have one serving, as it does contain an ounce of strong alcohol. Alternatively, order ice water with lemon, which will clear your palate for your next bite of food. Make sure that you are not wearing any undergarments under your outfit. The easy access to the body he has missed will drive him wild with desire. Let white curtains billow with full breezes. Change your bed sheets to cool, white linens. Place a white tablecloth over your dining table and fill your home with small, white candles. Place a small vase of daisies next to your bed.

Pulse Point Oil

ORANGE BLOSSOM

Dab orange blossom essential oil on the sheets and curtains and add one drop to the lightbulb in the bathroom. Your environment should have the scent; you should only smell clean.

How to Serve the Poem

Compose your own poem, or use the one at the beginning of the chapter. Rewrite this poem on a piece of stationery, seal it in an envelope, address it, and put a stamp on it. Mail it to yourself to get that dirty "just been through the postal system" appearance.

Menu

DINE OUT AT A FRENCH RESTAURANT, THEN SERVE FRESH, BLACK CAVIAR, AND ICED VODKA OR BALSAMIC VINEGAR TINCTURE

Eating caviar will make you both feel like royalty. You will want to recline among sumptuous pillows and feed each other tiny spoonfuls of this most luxurious food.

Activity
SLOW AND SEXY PARTNER YOGA

Yoga can be very sexy indeed—slow movements, stretches, reaches, and slow, sensual positions. Do some postures together and watch each other's bodies. You will begin to feel very aroused just watching each other. Your body will look so supple and fluid to him, he will be unable to concentrate. Ask him to assist you, and assist him as well. Trust each other's hands. You will find yourselves touching each other sensually before you know it. Stretch, soothe, relax, smile, be one with each other. Take the slow movements to a whole other level, and invent some positions of your own. If you are unfamiliar with Yoga, try these stretches:

Gentle Twist

Sit on the floor cross-legged, back to back. As you gently twist to the right, reach your hand around to touch your partners left knee. Put your left hand on your own right knee. Your partner will twist to his right and put his right hand on your left knee and his right hand on his own right knee. Do not strain, but hold the pose for a few moments breathing deeply.

Resting Pose

Have your partner sit on his heels, with his knees together. Now have him bend forward until his forehead touches the floor. Place your hands in the middle of his back and press gently. If he likes this, you can press harder, or even drape your body over his back. Have him come up slowly, and then change places.

The Morning After
LOX WITH CAPERS, HOT COFFEE

Prepare a lox platter and make very hot, fresh coffee and serve it in mismatched, antique cups and saucers. Take the meal either outside or next to a large window, where you can wake up at sunrise and watch the sun come up while you sip coffee and nibble on the salty lox slices. You can always go back to bed and sleep longer, but there is nothing sweeter than slow, sleepy lovemaking at first morning light. The salty taste of the lox will also put you both in the mood as the taste will remind you of sweaty skin at a very subtle level, much in the same way that touching each other after exercising is always very erotic.

RECIPES

Caviar

All caviar, whether fresh or pasteurized, should be thoroughly chilled. It can be purchased from a reputable grocer or gourmet shop. Good caviar usually costs about sixty to eighty dollars per ounce, but if you can find a good Russian deli, good Russian caviar will be about twenty to thirty dollars per ounce. Embed the serving bowl in ice or use a sculpted ice bowl (see instructions in part 3 of this book). You should keep some caviar in the back of your deli drawer for yourself, as it can be a wonderful pick-me-up at the end of a long, hard day when enjoyed with an ice-cold, imported beer.

No embellishments are really necessary for fresh caviar; however, you can try these simple extras if you would like to add a little excitement:

- Heap it on fresh, buttered toast. A nice soft, dark bread (toastettes), sliced thinly into small squares is ideal.
- Sprinkle a few drops of fresh lemon juice over it, followed by a tiny dollop of fresh cream fraiche, or sour cream. You may also try a drop of hot sauce.
- Eat it by the spoonful as the true connoisseur does.

Never use a metal utensil in caviar. A metal utensil will make the caviar turn instantly. There are spoons available that are made of shell or mother-of-pearl. These are ideal and very beautiful. You can also use a small wooden spoon as a substitute. Never, ever freeze caviar. Buy it the same day you plan to eat it if you can, and keep it in the back of the refrigerator until serving time.

If using pasteurized caviar, the best way to serve it is to make a spread with the pressed caviar, a little cream cheese, and enough sour cream to make it of spreading consistency. Spread on fingers of fresh white bread.

This erotic delicacy is best with ice-cold, fine Russian vodka. Kettle One is also extremely smooth. Try citron-flavored vodkas for a tangy flavor.

Balsamic Vinegar Tincture

In a chilled, tall glass combine:
Ice
Two or three drops fine quality balsamic or champagne vinegar

Fill with seltzer water.

Lox with Capers

Purchase good, sliced lox from a gourmet grocer and arrange it on a small, exquisite platter. Toss a few tiny capers around the slices, and a few small lemon wedges for squeezing.

The Afternoon Seduction

Poem
"I've Been Thinking about You"

Activity
Creamy Body Butter Treatment

Pulse Point
Body Butter

Color Scheme
Blue as the Afternoon Sky

Menu
Chicken Skewers with Mango Butter
and Pink Underpants Cocktail or
Sweet Peach Seltzer (nonalcoholic)

The Morning After
Crêpes and Strawberries

I've Been Thinking about You

I thought of you when I was in the shower last night.

I wished that the water running down my body was your hand instead.

You invaded my dreams while I slept so that when

I woke in the middle of the night I felt your lips on my skin and an

empty place beside me.

The sheets there were cold but I could still trace your

arms and back lightly in the air.

I want to feel your whole body against mine in the dark, and

hear your fast breathing.

I want you to reach for me and pull me to you and

I want this soon to be a reality,

not only a dream.

This seduction is for the middle of a weekend afternoon. Tell him to wear clothing that he does not mind getting messy, while you do the same. Enjoy your light lunch before you begin this smooth and sensuous treatment. You will feel vital and vigorous after enjoying your meal so that you may devote all of your attention to the activities at hand. You should enjoy your meal with the drapes open and bask in glorious, natural sunlight together. You may want to make love on the carpet when the sun is bright, and you can see out through the drapes but nobody can see in. This is the perfect way to experience exhibitionism.

Setting the Scene

Have the meal ready and waiting on a small, sun-dappled table by the window. Arrange the table sweetly with small vases of tiny garden flowers such as clover, dandelions, a few pretty grasses, and some small buds and berries. One way that I always like to decorate the afternoon table is with small ornate planting pots with fresh, growing moss in them. Moss can be easily transferred to a pot when given plenty of water and they will make your table look like a peaceful little garden. Any home repair warehouse can help you find the right pots and mosses; some are in pots, ready for sale. Wear a light, baby blue so that you will be as fresh as the sky outside, and try to find some dainty blue flowers for placing on the morning table.

Pulse Point

BODY BUTTER

Instead of a pulse point oil, you will be using the body butter, which smells of delicious tropical fruit. Rub a little on your hands before he arrives so he can encounter this tantalizing scent as soon as he walks in your door. You may dab a little vanilla fragrance oil on the bed pillows. This will touch your dreams with sensual sweetness.

How to Serve the Poem

Compose your own poem, or use the one at the beginning of the chapter. Wrap a thin ribbon of raffia around the second cocktail that you serve him and attach a small card with the poem on it. He will be reading it when he is feeling less nervous and, as a result, his imagination will run wild when he reads the poem.

Menu

CHICKEN SKEWERS WITH MANGO BUTTER AND PINK UNDERPANTS COCKTAIL OR SWEET PEACH SELTZER (NONALCOHOLIC)

These tasty items will not cause any uncomfortably full feeling, and will not make you drowsy. The vodka used in the cocktail will be easy on your system, as it is the purest alcohol made. Serve Sweet Peach Seltzer as an alternative.

Activity

CREAMY BODY BUTTER TREATMENT

The body butter can be a bit messy, so you will want to cover or remove clothing. Lay an old, pretty blanket on the carpet in the sunniest patch. Scoop some of the butter into a small stone jar, place it by the blanket, and leave a tiny butter knife in the bowl. It is much more pleasurable when used at room temperature. Roll up your sleeves and have him roll up his. Remove all watches and rings, or go ahead and remove all clothing altogether. Never allow yourself or your date to feel pressured. Scoop some of the butter with the knife and spread it onto your hands. Rub your hands together to warm and soften the butter. Slowly massage the butter into his hand and fingers. Work your way up to his wrists and arms, and shoulders and neck, if you're going that far. When done with the hands, start on the feet and legs if he's up for it. In both the hands and feet, there are many pleasure receptors and pressure points that can arouse and sooth your date effectively. Be slow and gentle, and make small circular movements. The body butter will melt into the skin to some degree, but some of it will stay on the skin, making you both slippery. If you have the time and inclination, go for the full-body experience, spreading more of the butter until you are both very aroused. The blanket will absorb the butter and make sure you do not make a mess. A shower will be in order afterward, but for the time being, act like a little child and revel in being slick and slimy. The butter is all natural, and is completely safe for playing in.

Tropical Dream Body Butter

3 tsp beeswax beads
¼ cup almond oil
¼ cup glycerin
20 drops each mango, peach, and lime perfume oil
2 drops each yellow and red food coloring

Melt beeswax in a small pan. In a separate pan, heat almond oil and glycerin. Stir into the beeswax. Remove from the heat, and place in a bowl. Whip with an electric mixer until well blended. Add oils and food coloring and blend well. Let cool for twenty minutes, and continue to whip until cool and thick. The body butter should never be put in the refrigerator.

The Morning After
Crêpes and Strawberries

If your afternoon delight turns into an all-night engagement, the next morning treat your date to a charming breakfast somewhere out of the way and quiet. Crêpes with fresh strawberries and freshly whipped cream will make you relive the creamy whipped experience of the day before. Enjoy other fresh morning pastries, and stroke each other's hands and fingers. Remember the massage and enjoy how soft the skin is as a result.

RECIPES

Chicken Skewers with Mango Butter

2 fresh, boneless, skinless chicken breasts cut into small pieces
2 thin slices fresh ginger root
2 tbsp peanut oil
1 small, white onion cut into small squares
salt
pepper
wooden skewers

Thread the chicken and onion onto the wooden skewers. Sauté the skewers in a shallow pan on medium heat with two tablespoons peanut oil, ginger root, salt, and pepper. Turn frequently until done. Test for doneness by piercing the chicken with a sharp knife. If the juice that flows is clear, the chicken is done. Arrange the skewers on the serving plate, and place in the fridge until ready to serve. Serve cold with the mango butter (almost as tasty as the body butter).

Mango Butter

¼ cup well-pureed mango
¼ cup unsalted sweet butter
dash of salt

Whip all ingredients in a blender at high speed until light and fluffy; serve immediately.

Pink Underpants Cocktail

In a large glass mix:
Ice
1 oz vodka (great quality only, Kettle One, if possible)

Fill with pink lemonade. Garnish with a maraschino cherry.

Sweet Peach Seltzer (nonalcoholic)

Rub the rims of two chilled champagne tulips with a lemon wedge and then run rims through a little powdered sugar. Fill half-full with chilled peach nectar sweetened with a teaspoon of honey, and then fill with seltzer water. Garnish with a slice of fresh peach.

The Luscious Seduction

Poem
"I'll Show You All of Me"

Activity
Rose Spa Bath

Pulse Point Oil
Rose

Color Scheme
Fresh Yellow

Menu
Frozen Fruits and
Mai Tai Cocktails or Virgin
Ginger Tart (nonalcoholic)

The Morning After
Rose Petal Tea

I'll Show You All of Me

Black fog, so alive,

Come and charm my skin.

Cause muscle to tense and my blood to thicken

Because you're my passion that haunts me, I know,

When you brush my face and my bosom so slow.

You lift through my blouse and tease my flesh,

heat my desire with every caress.

'Til I need you to touch me, ignore my resolve,

and let you please me as the night moves on.

Enjoy my body with your hands and tongue.

Push up against me, and I know we've begun.

Show me your body when you're hard and tensed,

and drink of my lips 'til your thirst is quenched.

I'm weak to resist you and you begin the game.

Play me please, for I need it again.

Forever I'll want it and I'll always yearn,

awake every night until you return.

*U*se this seduction later at night, after dinnertime, at about 9:00 P.M. Make sure you tell him to eat dinner before he comes over. This seduction is very intimate when your relationship has reached a new level. You will show your insecurities and passion without seeming weak or clingy. Use this chapter for the total realization and gratification of your love. If the next level of the relationship is to be achieved, certain truths must be shared, such as how you feel about his body, and how he will respond to the lusts that you have for him. The dark side of this poem is important as it shows an unstoppable and almost unearthly attraction to each other. A tendency to be a bit dark is always very enticing to a man as it means that you are not afraid of this side of yourself. He will know that your actions in bed will be more deep and honest as well.

Setting the Scene

Buy a dozen yellow roses and pluck off most of the petals, saving one or two full flowers. Scatter petals on the floor, on and in the sheets, on the bathroom floor, and in the tub. Scoop some into bowls and keep them beside pillows or near a lamp where the heat will release their fragrance. Scoop more into a pretty bowl and place it by the tub. Toss a few petals on your sheets and pillows, too.

Light ten or more candles, all in a straight row in the bathroom, and place one candle in each corner of the bath tub. These should provide enough light to see each other very well. Have light cello music playing in the background. Place a large ladle, wooden if possible, and a large sea sponge by the tub.

Burn a stick of sweet incense (one-fourth of a stick only if your bathroom is small). One stick of honey and one of rose should make the perfect scent. If the incense is too hard to find, use candles that are made of pure beeswax. They will smell just like honey.

Pulse Point Oil

ROSE

Dab a drop of rose oil under each pillow on the bed. Also dab a tiny bit behind your knees, as the scent will rise upward when you get hot.

How to Serve the Poem

Compose your own poem, or use the one at the beginning of the chapter. Present this poem on a small white card with a rose petal inside and a drop of rose oil on the back of the card to remind him on later days. You should be barely dressed at the time. Men are always more receptive when they are confronted with a scantily clad woman. Any insecurity he has about showing his feelings will vanish.

Menu
FROZEN FRUITS AND MAI TAI COCKTAILS OR VIRGIN GINGER TART
Frozen fruits make delicious, sensual little treats that you can have fun with, and they aren't as heavy as a dessert. Go ahead, indulge!

Activity
ROSE SPA BATH
Phone your date and tell him to let himself in, as the door will be unlocked. You will be waiting in the bathroom, sitting on the edge of the tub with a rose in your lap. Draw a very hot bath with the fizzing powder (recipe follows). It will let off a delicious fragrance as the tub fills up. The water should be hotter than you would like. Your skin can adjust to hot water but water that is even a little bit too cold will ruin the evening. Toss in just a few of the rose petals so they will let off some fragrance in the hot water as you wait for your date.

Sip the mai tai as you both playfully undress each other and then ease each other into the bath, which should still be very hot. Toss more rose petals into the bath water as you get in and sit down facing each other. Hopefully, you have a bathtub that can accommodate two people. If not, you will need to spoon each other to fit in. Once you are comfortable, take a few minutes to feel the hot water and enjoy how your wet skin feels against his. Enjoy how his skin smells. Soak up the hot water and begin to feel your limbs get a little sluggish. Use the ladle to pour water over each other, and gently run the water over yourselves with the sponge. This should be done very slowly and sensually. Concentrate on the shoulders and chest as these areas will feel as though they are being massaged. Place some of the rose petals over your chest and breasts. Enjoy the mai tai and some frozen fruits in the bath. The bath should take no longer than twenty minutes. A longer bath will make you drowsy.

Afterwards, snuggle up in fat, fluffy robes while still wet from the tub. You will air dry soon enough, and you must not take the attention off of each other even to dry off.

Fizzing Bath Powder

½ cup baking soda
¼ cup cornstarch
¼ cup citric acid (vitamin C powder)
20 drops grapefruit, apple, peach, or freesia essential oil
A few drops yellow food coloring

Mix food colorings together in a small bowl. Combine dry ingredients in a blender or food processor. Add food coloring and mix well. Add oil and blend. Place in large, colorful jar. Sprinkle two to three tablespoons of salts over hot bath water just before getting in.

The Morning After
ROSE PETAL TEA

Roses are edible and can be very healthful. They are also known for their calming properties. For rose petal tea, simply add a couple of crushed rose petals to a favorite loose tea. Remember to wash the petals first. Peppermint tea and lemon tea are the most compatible with the subtle rose flavor. Use one heaping teaspoonful for every eight ounces of water. Add hot water and let steep five minutes, then strain and serve. When serving the tea, place one rose petal on the saucer and a raw sugar cube on the side of the saucer, and use the loveliest tea cups you can find.

RECIPES

Frozen Fruits

Select small fruits such as grapes, blueberries, raspberries, or any other small, sweet berry that is in season. Freeze them in freezer bags the day before. A tiny bit of freshly whipped cream can be used as a dip for these. Also, for a sweet and playfully sticky topping, try some warm honey drizzled on top. As the honey gets colder, it will harden a bit, giving a toffee-like consistency.

Mai Tai Cocktails

Chill two large hurricane glasses.

In a large glass combine:
Ice
½ oz triple sec
1 oz light rum
½ oz creme de almond

Fill with ½ pineapple juice and ½ orange juice. Transfer drink into chilled hurricane glass to mix. Top each glass with one-half ounce Myers dark rum, and garnish with maraschino cherries.

Virgin Ginger Tart

In a large glass combine:
Ice

Fill with ½ sweet and sour mix and ½ ginger ale. Transfer to chilled serving glass.

Rose Petal Tea

Wash several rose petals and crush them with the back of a spoon. Mix the petals with a favorite loose tea (peppermint and lemon teas are the most compatible with the subtle rose flavor).

A Lovely Daydream

Poem
"I Dreamt of You"

Activity
Watch the Clouds and Daydream

Pulse Point Oil
Sun-Warmed Lavender

Color Scheme
Spring Fresh Peach

Menu
Stuffed Snails, Fruit, Cheese, and
Midori Sour Cocktails and
Dry White Wine or Grapefruit
Frappé (nonalcoholic)

The Morning After
Eggs Benedict

I Dreamt of You

In a dream, I follow you in secret.

I match your footsteps so you'll not know of my presence.

My shadow dances behind you,

but I am actually before you,

awaiting your approach,

watching every movement, and

your breath warm and constant.

See your own reflection in my eyes,

standing naked, and look deeper.

I will show you other dreams.

Until then you will not know how far they go.

But dreams are not real,

and not to be lived in.

I ask why I should dream at all,

and in a dream,

from shadows,

you answer.

You will charm him right out of his reservations. This picnic is sweet, suggestive, pure, inventive, and memorable. This will stay alive in his memory forever as one of the best afternoons of his life. It is perfect in every way. Every man has seen picnics like this in his mind. The sun is warm but not hot, the breeze ruffles your blouse and hair, you rest your head on his lap to enjoy the slowly passing clouds. You are both calm, having eaten delicacies. You sip buttery wine, and let the day ease by while lazing on an old, soft blanket. You hear sounds far away and only feel the present. Perfect.

Setting the Scene

Rent a convertible for the weekend. Test it yourself for maneuverability so that you will be comfortable driving it. The site should be a surprise to him, a place that he has never seen before. You will need to stake out the site beforehand. Take the scenic route to the picnic site and enjoy the ride. Go to nearby lakes, parks, and other woody areas to find your perfect picnic site. The hood of the car may prove a perfect place to recline. Check the weather first. Any day will work well, but a Sunday before a Monday holiday from work is ideal. It reminds us of the things that we can be extra grateful for. We tend to be lazier on days such as this, and more willing to accept the day's peacefulness. On your picnic, talk only of fanciful things, dreams, and the things you like most. Wear your most fluttery skirt or dress. If it happens to breeze and lift your skirt up to reveal either tiny lace panties, or, better yet, no underwear at all, all the better for you. You are nature's nymph, after all.

Pulse Point Oil

Sun-Warmed Lavender
In a small perfume bottle combine:
20 drops lavender oil
5 drops peach oil
2 drops vanilla oil
An equal amount jojoba oil if using pure essential oils.

Let sit overnight to let the scents marry. Dab on pulse points. Also dab a tiny amount on your hairbrush and run through your hair, starting with the ends, as the oil will not only prove more fragrant, but the benefits of oil are easier on the dry ends of hair rather than close to the scalp.

How to Serve the Poem

Compose your own poem, or use the one at the beginning of the chapter. Write the poem on a small, patterned piece of tissue-like paper. Antique drawer lining papers work nicely as they also often have a pleasant fragrance. Another option is to use a warm iron to press dried, wild flowers between two pieces of wax paper with the poem, on paper, in the middle. Run the iron over it several times and flatten it in a phone book if it curls. Place the poem inside the picnic basket and ask him to open it when you are ready to have your meal.

Menu

Stuffed Snails, Fruit, Cheese, and Midori Sour Cocktails and Dry White Wine or Grapefruit Frappé

Pack a picnic basket with the courses in sequence. Place the snails on the bottom, followed by the fruit and cheese, and top with the thermos of cocktails. Place the folded napkins and utensils on top of the whole thing, and do not forget items like the corkscrew, cheese knife, and snail forks. You may also want to pack Wet-Naps, as you may be messy by the end of the meal.

Activity

Watch the Clouds and Daydream

All that is required of you is that you relax your body and let the day entertain you. When you have eaten, recline on each other and think in silence for a moment. Breathe and concentrate on breathing deeper and slower. Let your body become one with the rhythm of the earth. Only when you feel serene should you feel the urge to share your thoughts. Your conversation will be pure and honest. Speak of your likes, loves, and what kind of places you wish to visit one day. Feel the warmth of each other, and bask in the glow of sharing your dreams.

The Morning After

Eggs Benedict

Wake up late, shower slowly, get dressed without trying to match, and maybe wear a hat. Drive to a beachfront café, or, if you do not have a beach, your favorite café will do nicely. Enjoy fresh French roast coffee and eggs benedict with freshly made hollandaise sauce. Spend the morning being free and do whatever tickles your fancy.

RECIPES

Stuffed Snails

Even if you have tried snails and did not like them, I would urge you to give them another try. Yes, they are odd, and, of course, they are snails. Try to not think of them as snails. They are a delicacy, and it is the strange texture and unfamiliarity that makes them so seductive. Purchase escargot holders from a fine-cooking store. They look like metal paint-mixing pallettes. Prepare these immediately before you leave for the picnic.

¼ tsp minced garlic

5 tbsp butter

2 tbsp chopped parsley

½ tsp salt

Dash of fresh pepper

¾ cup soft, fresh bread crumbs

1 can French snails

1 bay leaf

½ tsp fresh thyme

2 parsley sprigs

2 tbsp dry white wine

24 snail shells

Preheat oven to 450° F. Sauté garlic in three tablespoons of the butter for about four minutes, and remove from heat. Add parsley, half of the salt, the pepper, and the breadcrumbs. Mix lightly. Empty the snails with their liquid into the saucepan, and add the bay leaf, thyme, parsley, and wine. Cover and simmer for ten minutes. Drain and cool slightly. Melt the rest of the butter and combine it with the rest of the salt. Dip each snail into this mixture and nestle it into a shell. Fill the rest of the shell with the bread-crumb mixture (about one-half teaspoon each). Set into snail holders and bake for 6 to 8 minutes.

Fruit and Cheese

Arrange stacks of thin water crackers with slices of Brie, Camembert, Gruyere, Gorgonzola, Feta, Gouda, aged sharp cheddar, Edam, paper-thin slices of Swiss Lace, Muenster, and chunks of blue cheese. Wrap in plastic wrap. Arrange slices of fruits such as red apple, ripe fig, pear, and halved small apricots on a small dish and cover with plastic as well. The fruit and cheese should be eaten together, and, of course, the milder cheeses, such as the Feta, Edam, Gouda, Swiss, and Gruyere, should be drizzled with a little clover honey and fed to your date. Bring a small honey pot for this purpose. A fabulous way to enjoy honey with cheese is to prepare the honey with fresh lemon juice. Adjust the amount of juice to taste. The lemon juice gives just the right tartness to the super sweet, and enhances the flavor of the milder cheeses.

Midori Sour Cocktails
In a metal mixing cup combine:
Ice
2 oz Midori
4 oz sweet and sour mix

Shake and strain in the glasses. Garnish with a mint cherry (or two). If you do not like this particular cocktail, bring a fine, dry white wine instead. A buttery wine will go very well with the snails, and should be chilled a bit before heading out.

Pour the Midori Sour Cocktail into a thermos to keep cold, and bring two cocktail glasses.

Grapefruit Frappé
In a blender combine:
1 cup ice
1 cup fresh grapefruit juice
2 tbsp confectioner's sugar
1 tbsp grenadine

Blend until pureed and smooth. Transfer to a thermos. The ice will melt but it will keep the drink very cold.

The Welcoming Seduction

Poem
"I've Been Ready for You"

Activity
Candlelight Portraits

Pulse Point Oil
Venus Perfume Oil

Color Scheme
Red and Purple

Menu
Giant Shrimp Cocktail and
Black Orchid Cocktail
or Shirley Temples

The Morning After
Fresh Croissants and Tea

I've Been Ready for You

Your mouth on my neck makes light of my resisting.

I can't turn away from you. I am your prey

and you kiss me with hunger that's pure passion and ferocity.

You'll keep me embraced forever.

The need to touch you keeps me here.

You don't have to try hard to keep my lust, do you?

You are the wild creature that watches me, tracks me, and waits

until I am naked and I am wanting.

You approach and hold me still with those eyes.

I am still unwilling to move.

My body tells me that I need it.

Now that you've got me, what are you going to do with me?

*I*f you are ready to get physical, ready to hear the truth, ready to know all about each other, or if you are ready to try something new in bed, try this seduction. Afterwards, get dressed into comfortable clothing and go out for dinner at a family-owned Italian restaurant where you can have some rich red wine with your angel hair pomodoro with feta (a wonderful, light meal). Make sure that the restaurant has red-and-white-checkered tablecloths, fresh bread, and great Italian music.

Setting the Scene

Adorn the table by your bed with as many red tulips as you can find—two or three dozen ought to be enough. Use purple accessories to deepen the impact of the red. Red is a passionate color, but when paired with a deep, royal purple or violet, it has ten times the impact. For example: have a couple of purple candles, or drink out of purple glasses, or have purple napkins or place mats on the table. These colors will give you both a sense that you are staying in an international inn. Your own home will be unfamiliar, and that will make you both feel more open to new things.

Instead of using candles, get a small oil lamp and place it on your windowsill. Find the kind with the wind guard that surrounds the flame. It should have a knob on the side of the wick, used to raise and the lower the flame. You can start off with more light and move on to using less. If you have a fireplace, use that instead. Leave the window open even if it is cold. The flame will be warm, and the chill will give you a reason to curl up together under a thick down comforter and many soft pillows.

If you can find a large, square or rectangular piece of beautifully colored fabric, you can use it to create a tent-style ceiling to your bed. A bright buttercup yellow will brighten every morning; but, for this seduction you may want to use a sheer orangey-red. Use a wide-topped nail to affix the center of the fabric to the ceiling at the center of your bed. Affix the other four corners to the ceiling over the four corners of your bed or a little past. Make sure that the fabric billows down from the center. You can hang tassels from the four corners if you wish.

Put on soft music. Try some reed flute. There's no reason why you cannot turn your living room into a harem tent if you so desire; let your imagination be your guide. You can always change it back later. Keep your outfit light and sheer if possible (totally sheer if you are very close with your date). I like the combination of conservative slacks with a sheer blouse and no bra. Wear a blazer to the restaurant unless you are very daring. For lips, use only a dab of very shiny, pale pink or peach lip gloss. These light touches will contrast and add sweetness to the rich colors you are using.

Pulse Point Oil

VENUS PERFUME OIL

To follow is a recipe for a homemade perfume. Add a drop or two to the liquid wax in the top of each candle by the bed or on the dining table. Also, add a drop to a lightbulb in a lamp. I like to use this for the lamp in the bathroom.

Venus Perfume Oil

¾ tsp sandalwood essential oil
12 drops each rose and jasmine essential oils
½ tsp jojoba oil

Place essential oils in a one-fourth ounce perfume vial. Add jojoba oil. Cap it and shake to blend. Let sit overnight to marry the essences. This is a wonderful scent to add to a bath, or use as bath oil by diluting it with turkey red oil. This is one of my favorite scents, so you can imagine that I use a good deal of it.

The next time you go to his place, bring a plain, white candle and scent it by adding a drop or two to the pool of wax at the base of the wick. It will remind him of you every time he lights it.

How to Serve the Poem

Compose your own poem, or use the one at the beginning of the chapter. Write the poem on a blank card. Write his name on the back of it and place it on a bed pillow. Place a single, expensive truffle on the card. This will let him know your intentions ahead of time so he can start thinking of ways to please you.

Menu

GIANT SHRIMP COCKTAIL AND BLACK ORCHID COCKTAIL OR SHIRLEY TEMPLES

Play with the shrimp. Feed each other. Drink the cocktails by a breezy window with a great view, or on a great blanket on the carpet. The exotic cocktail will add to the visually arresting environment. Certainly use the tulips for tickling, and above all, be comfortable with how sweet and beautiful you look so you can fully enjoy yourself. Admire your curves in a mirror for a little while before the date.

Activity
CANDLELIGHT PORTRAITS

Make portraits of each other by candlelight. Buy charcoals in warm colors ranging from yellow to dark chestnut brown and black. Any art store will have the charcoals and good paper. These supplies are inexpensive. Use candles on the floor to shadow and highlight your best features. Use the black to highlight the darkest areas. Try only to concentrate on the light and shadow against the shape of your bodies. You may wish to sketch the side of his face or chest and he may wish to sketch your buttocks, hips, or breasts. Whether or not either of you are any good at this, it is a definite turn on for the creative romantic. Your ability may surprise you.

The Morning After
FRESH CROISSANTS AND TEA

Purchase croissants in the morning before your man awakens. Any local bakery should make them fresh and early, but you may wish to do some research beforehand to be sure of your source. Enjoy a distinctly flavored tea such as Earl Grey to compliment the rich, buttery texture of the croissants. A delicious variation is to add milk and honey to your tea. Many find it a terrific alternative to morning coffee.

RECIPES

Giant Shrimp Cocktail

Choose very large tiger shrimp from a good seafood vendor. It is very convenient to purchase a bag of frozen, precooked shrimp. All that is required of you is that you thaw and wash them. Cover and refrigerate them until ready to serve. Expect that each of you won't eat more than ten shrimp, or five of the very huge U-6s. (This is a common way of measuring shrimp and other kinds of small seafood. It means that you need less than six of them to make a pound). The kind of glasses that ice cream sundaes are served in, at old-fashioned malt shops, are perfect for shrimp cocktail. They hold the cocktail sauce while providing a pleasing rim for the shrimp to be arranged on. Prepare one glass for each of you, and place the shrimp on the edge of the glass with the tail facing outward and curled over the rim. Place a lemon wedge, twisted, in each glass and add a sprig of parsley.

Perfect Cocktail Sauce

1 ½ cups ketchup
2 tbsp horseradish
1 small red onion, grated
juice of 1 lemon
dash or two of Tabasco sauce
1 tsp garlic powder
½ tsp paprika

Mix all ingredients in a small bowl. Refrigerate until ready to serve. Shrimp are best when eaten with the fingers, and this is the perfect opportunity to hand-feed each other and be appropriately flirtatious. Bottled cocktail sauce can be very suitable, but if you have the time, I recommend making it fresh. This recipe is my favorite; you can always add more horseradish if you prefer a hotter sauce. Bear in mind that spicy foods warm the body, make the face flush, and make the body excited.

Black Orchid Cocktail

In a blender combine::
Crushed ice for two glasses
1 oz vodka
1 oz Blue Curacao
2 oz cranberry juice

Blend. Pour into two tulip glasses. Top with orange juice and lime juice.

Shirley Temple

A great alternative if you do not want alcohol. Add a dash of grenadine to a glass of lemon-lime soda. Garnish with two thin red straws and maraschino cherries.

The Sweet Seduction

Poem
"Every Reason"

Activity
Smile for the Camera

Pulse Point Oil
Sweet Violet

Color Scheme
Deep, Deep Purple

Menu
Chocolate Fondue and
Chocolate Chip Cookie Cocktails
or Honey Water (nonalcoholic)

The Morning After
Vanilla Poached Pears and Café Latte

Every Reason

The way you charm me and never lie,

Makes me feel sexy, and that is why,

I need you.

Because you hug me and hold me tight,

I wake up lonely, and every night,

I want you.

And with every moment,

of every day,

For every reason, and

In every way,

I love you.

*T*his is a Valentine's Day seduction. It can otherwise be used for making any occasion sweet—the day you decide to move in together, the day he gets promoted at work, or any special day. You can also use this seduction for saying "I love you," for the very first time.

Setting the Scene

After you enjoy dinner at a tiny, local restaurant, walk along the beach or through a park. You could also walk around barefoot in your backyard, slowly crushing the grass and making fists with your toes, holding each other's hands and looking for clovers and fluffy dandelion puffs. Dress in the darkest, deepest, most sinful purple you can find. A satin slip dress works well, or simply add a purple piece to your favorite black suit, such as a deep purple suede camisole, or purple suede stiletto heels (my personal favorite). To use shades of purple in the home, limit the addition to shocking purple cut crystal stemware for the table, or a set of purple salad plates to top your daily favorites. One large, purple leather pillow will carry almost any color scheme nicely. Buy a single, red rose for the evening, and put it in a tiny vase by your bed. Maybe later you'll want to pluck off a petal or two and tickle his bare chest.

Pulse Point Oil

SWEET VIOLET

For sweet violet oil, combine five drops of violet oil with two drops of frangipani oil. Add an equal amount of jojoba oil if using pure essential oils. Dab the oil on your pulse points, and add a drop to the liquid wax in your bedside candle.

How to Serve the Poem

Compose your own poem, or use the one at the beginning of the chapter. Write this poem on a small note card and place it among the petals of the rose. He will notice it as soon as you lead him to your bed.

Menu

CHOCOLATE FONDUE AND CHOCOLATE CHIP COOKIE COCKTAILS OR HONEY WATER

Dip, sip, talk deeply, and kiss the taste of the cocktails off of each other's lips.

Activity
SMILE FOR THE CAMERA

You will seduce each other by making you both into movie stars of the big screen. Use black and white film, and, preferably, an antique camera. You can find some great antique cameras at pawnshops. Take him to your bedroom in the sunlight by the window shades. Wrap him up in them and take a picture of his hair blowing across his forehead. He will take pictures of you lying across the arms of a chair, or reclining, scantily clad, on a large, luxurious trench coat or velvet wrap. Press your hair against your cheek and smile like you are the breath of springtime. You are the flower goddess, and he is the boy-prince of the county. Be whatever you wish; this is your time and your fantasy. Some people develop a real love for developing their own film in a darkroom. Although, if you would like to take more risqué pictures and wish to have privacy, I would suggest you invest in a Polaroid camera. Just make sure that you keep the photos in a safe place.

The Morning After
VANILLA POACHED PEARS AND CAFÉ LATTE

If you have any film left over from the night before, go ahead and use it up now. After enjoying your pears and café latte, you may want to stroll down to the one-hour photo development place and walk around or sit quietly on a bench reading the paper together until your photos are developed.

RECIPES

Chocolate Fondue

⅓ cup whipping cream
8 oz bittersweet chocolate chips

Bring whipping cream to a simmer in a small, heavy saucepan. Reduce heat to low and add the chocolate chips. Whisk until smooth. Transfer fondue to a fondue pot and place over its candle. Serve with one-inch cubes of pound cake, cheesecake, or angel food cake. Also serve with fresh-hulled strawberries, pear slices, banana pieces, and other small fruits.

Chocolate Chip Cookie Cocktail

In a metal mixing cup combine:
Ice
¾ oz Frangelico
¼ oz White Crème de Cocoa
½ oz cream

Shake and strain into an old-fashioned glass with ice. Top with whip cream and shaved chocolate or finely crushed Oreo cookie powder. This topping is great on ice cream as well.

It is always a great idea to keep a mixture of Frangelico, White Crème de Cocoa, and coffee creamer in a bottle in your refrigerator. Add an ounce to your coffee every morning if you like. For a sweeter syrup, add an ounce or two of light corn syrup and stir well before bottling.

Honey Water

In a large, chilled glass combine:
Ice
1 tsp honey
2 drops rose infusion
1 drop orange water
Fill with ice water

The rose infusion and orange water are available at most fine liquor stores. They are nonalcoholic, but many use them to delicately flavor water and tea.

Vanilla Poached Pears

2 fresh pears, peeled, halved, and seeded
½ cup white corn syrup
¼ cup Frangelico
2 tsp vanilla extract
¼ cup butter
¼ cup water

Combine all ingredients except pears in a small saucepan and bring to a simmer. Place the pear halves in the pot so that they are all covered. Let simmer for thirty minutes or so. Turn the pears over and continue to simmer for another ten minutes. Remove from heat, transfer to a bowl, and cover with plastic until ready to use. To serve, place two pear halves on a tiny saucer, one overlapping the other. Top with reserved sauce.

Café Latte

A café latte is one ounce of espresso and at least four ounces of steamed milk. To make this, you will need an espresso machine with a steam attachment. You can otherwise add hot milk to very strong coffee. For strong coffee, use a regular amount of coffee grounds, but only four ounces of water (for two people).

The Sensual Seduction

Poem

"My Body Needs You"

Activity

Just a Little Strip Tease

Pulse Point Oil

Luscious Freesia and Tart Apple

Color Scheme

Flesh Colors

Menu

Frogs' Legs Appetizer
with Chardonnay or
Virgin Peach Fuzzy

The Morning After

Simple Poached Eggs and Heartwarming Tea

My Body Needs You

Throbbing.

Through me.

In me.

Over me.

Strange things that I feel, coursing through me,

making my breasts hot, my thighs impatient.

I soar through the day feeling everything, and

watching people and how they can feel nothing.

I don't understand my dreams but I know they are my passions.

I dream of thin wooden bridges, dark rooms and familiar people and

overwhelming, consuming kisses and caresses that warm all my skin.

I remember when I wake up.

I imagine over and over again.

It lives with me all day, making me desire what I wouldn't had I not dreamt it.

Before I fall asleep I will try to influence my dreams,

think of warmth, a fire, smooth hands on me,

soft lips just barely touching.

Deep, dark eyes that I sink into and

desire and want and begin.

$\mathcal{T}$his seduction will have him begging for your attention. You are proud of your body. You know your curves drive him insane with desire. Make sure he knows that you can see right through him. Tell him you can tell exactly what he wants you to do to him. Make him tell you what he wants to do to you. Tell each other little stories about sexual encounters you've heard about. Maybe you would like to try them? After tonight, he will see you every time he closes his eyes. Remember to wait thirty minutes after eating to begin any strenuous activity.

Setting the Scene

Lay a soft covering on a loveseat or soft chair and put a few small candles on the side table or coffee table. For the pure luxury, you may wish to buy a fake fur throw. They are large and sinful and lush, and they are a joy to touch. Please do not buy a genuine fur. Avoid direct lighting; use small lamps instead. You should set the table with a colorful tablecloth as well as many small candles and some loose flower buds around the plates. Use fleshy nude colors in your outfit and home. I had a leather dress made out of the perfect nude-colored leather. It is tight in all the right places. You should have a nude bodysuit for use under a prim and proper suit so that from a few feet away, it looks as though you are not wearing anything under your blazer. This outfit will also work nicely for this seduction, especially if the bodysuit is sheer in nature. Listen to light opera or French music while sipping the chardonnay before starting on the frogs' legs, as they will be more fun if you are a little bit tipsy.

Pulse Point Oil

LUSCIOUS FREESIA AND TART APPLE

Combine ten drops of freesia oil with three drops of apple oil, one drop of cucumber oil, and one drop of lilac oil. Add an equal amount of jojoba oil, as always. Let sit overnight to marry the scents. Apply to pulse points with a cotton swab. Add one drop to the lightbulb in the bathroom.

How to Serve the Poem

Compose your own poem, or use the one at the beginning of the chapter. The poem should be recited verbally after the meal. Start some smooth music, continuing with the French music if you can. Make sure that the only light is provided by five or so candles surrounding where he is sitting, preferably on the love seat in the living room.

Menu
FROGS' LEGS APPETIZER AND CHARDONNAY OR VIRGIN PEACH FUZZY

Play footsie while nibbling the frogs' legs and sipping chilled chardonnay or virgin peach fuzzies. Rub thin slices of sourdough baguette with a peeled, cut garlic clove, and use the bread to dip in the sauce on the platter. Enjoy this seduction as a light dinner. It will energize you.

Activity
JUST A LITTLE STRIP TEASE

When you have changed into a negligee, or some other tiny, handmade silk arrangement, cover yourself with a sheer robe. Come into the room and blow out one of the candles. Say a couple lines of the poem, blow out another candle, and remove an item. Continue along that same vein until you are completely naked, then sit on his lap and recite the rest of the poem. This strip tease is very easy and very hot. Try it. It will have quite an impact.

The Morning After
SIMPLE POACHED EGGS AND HEARTWARMING TEA

Make sure that you have the negligee from the night before in a place where he will see it, and remember your little tease. Wear something equally impressive as you enjoy breakfast together. The eggs are very clean tasting, and do not weigh on the stomach, so the two of you should be more than ready to enjoy some midmorning romping around your place.

RECIPES

French Country Frogs' Legs

8 jumbo frogs legs, trimmed
Milk
Seasoned flour for dredging
Peanut oil
1 tbsp butter
⅓ garlic clove, finely chopped
Dash of lemon juice
Dash of finely chopped parsley

Soak frogs' legs in water to cover for two hours. Drain and dry well. Dip the frogs' legs in milk, and then dredge in the seasoned flour (season flour by adding salt, pepper, cayenne, paprika, and thyme). Add peanut oil to a skillet to the depth of one-fourth of an inch. When it is hot, cook the frogs' legs on each side five to six minutes. Transfer to a hot platter and pour off the excess oil from the skillet. Add the butter to the skillet, and cook to a golden brown. Add the garlic, then pour over the frogs' legs. Arrange the frog legs on a decorative platter with lemon wedges and parsley. Sprinkle with lemon juice and parsley and serve immediately.

Virgin Peach Fuzzy

In a chilled wine glass combine:
1 slice of fresh peach
2 oz peach nectar
Fill with ice cold ginger ale

Simple Poached Eggs

3 tbsp white vinegar
1 tsp salt
2 eggs, at room temperature
water

Heat one inch of water with the vinegar and salt. Bring to a boil and reduce heat immediately. Break each egg into a saucer and slip carefully into the water. Let cook until the whites are firm. Remove the eggs from the water using a slotted spoon and let dry on paper towels. Trim to a circular shape with a cookie cutter. Top with butter and pepper and serve.

Heartwarming Tea

This recipe is absolutely pleasing; make some for yourself and keep it handy, as you will drink it often.

2 cups spearmint leaves, dry and finely chopped

¾ cups dried lemon peel

2 tbsp candied gingerroot, finely diced

½ cup cloves

1 tbsp anise seeds

Mix all the ingredients well, and place in a large tea jar. Keep it by your stove, the warmth will only enhance the flavors. To make: use one teaspoon per person plus an extra teaspoon for the pot, and let steep in boiling water for five minutes. Strain into teacups. Serve with raw sugar cubes and a twist of lemon rind.

The Playful Seduction

Poem
"Closer, Closer, and Almost"

Activity
Amusement Park Play Date

Pulse Point Oil
Glittering Solid Amber Perfume

Color Scheme
Fuchsia and Tropical Flowers

Menu
Ginger Cake and Shock Cocktails
with Candied Lemon Rind or
Lively Lime Wine Seltzer (nonalcoholic)

The Morning After
Breakfast Brownies and Creamy Raspberry Cocoa

Closer, Closer, and Almost

Circle my breasts with your open mouth and fingertips.

Move slowly, touch slowly.

Breathe with me.

Press your chest to mine

but don't give in to passion yet.

I'll let my hair fall over you.

My lips will speak to your skin in hot whispers.

My hands will move on you while yours search through me and

explore me; use your fingers.

My eyes will look into you,

our faces nearly touching,

our lips almost caressing, almost seeking, almost devouring.

Only a few moments of sweet, motionless sex before we begin.

Breathe, sweat.

Tease, and taste me.

Let all time pass us.

This seduction will awaken the desire in your date. It touches on all the primitive aspects of sexual actions. The finger food, the tangy sour cocktail—these things bring out the animal in men. This seduction will start the sex long before you get into the bedroom. Keep touching each other throughout the entire date until you get home. He may want to go home early. When you are out, start touching his hands, arms, and stomach first; later move on to more erotic areas like his neck, chest, legs, buttocks, thighs, lips. Place both hands on his sides and stroke up and down a couple of times. This will remind him of having sex and will excite him terribly. Place his hands on you as well. He will take the initiative and think up wonderful new things from there.

Setting the Scene

Before the day of the date, send him a letter with a poem. This will make him unbearably excited. Tell him of the amusement park, and what you might do to him on various rides. Send him some flowers such as large sunflowers, or good-sized orchids, and his coworkers will be terribly jealous. Wear something loose and comfortable in a bright, candy-like fuchsia, but don't wear anything under it. It'll drive your date crazy if they can't see any signs of bra or panty lines and they catch the occasional sign of a nipple. Wear a slick, nude-colored lip gloss. Pin a large, fuchsia tropical flower in your hair—hibiscus are lovely, but a couple of foxgloves will be extraordinary. If you do not have a fuchsia outfit, have a manicure and pedicure in a matte fuchsia instead.

Pulse Point Oil

Amber Perfume

Try this wonderful recipe for the perfect, travel-friendly, solid perfume. You can try it without glitter as well. Rub it on your cleavage crease, along your neck bones, and on the apples of your cheeks.

Glittering Solid Amber Perfume

½ tsp beeswax
3 ½ tsp grape seed oil
¾ tsp amber perfume oil
1 tsp loose gold sparkles (the finer the powder, the better)

Heat the grape seed oil in the microwave for two minutes, and remove. Then melt the beeswax completely in the microwave. Pour the oil into the wax. Allow to cool slightly. Add the amber oil and the sparkles quickly and stir. Immediately pour it into a cute little jar or container. This perfume travels well in a purse, and the sparkles look terrific in candlelight or while catching the moonlight.

How to Serve the Poem

Compose your own poem, or use the one at the beginning of the chapter. Write the poem on the front page of a small, thin, leather journal. It will show that you plan to add to it in the future. Later, include any feelings or thoughts you had during and after dinner. Later in the evening, once you are cozy at your place, give him the journal and a classy gift pen so that he may add to it, and perhaps write you a little verse. You can also sprinkle some gold dust into the journal and spray the area lightly with hair spray, which will help it stick.

Menu

GINGER CAKE AND SHOCK COCKTAILS WITH CANDIED LEMON RIND OR LIVELY LIME WINE SELTZER (NONALCOHOLIC)

The candied lemon rind is meant to be used for garnishing the cocktails, but you can certainly have fun with it. Tease his lips with it before letting him have a bite, or hold it in your teeth and let him share it with you. He must kiss you, or he does not deserve the candy.

Activity

AMUSEMENT PARK PLAY DATE

Have a late lunch at your place before leaving for the amusement park. The games, laughter, and childish rides will energize. The Ferris wheel has unlimited playful potential. Be a child. Be free. Give in to your laughter. Act like you always wanted to. Eat cotton candy or a frozen banana (something he will definitely enjoy watching). Play all the games you always feel too grown up to play. Twirl in the tea cup ride. Blow him kisses throughout the afternoon and whisper things that you would like to do to him. Maybe act some of those things out at the top of the Ferris wheel. Do not be ashamed of any simple, silly desire you have; just give in to it. He will see the joy in your eyes and be drawn to you. After much gaming and flirting, you will be hungry enough to have dinner at a nearby restaurant before going back to your place for dessert and treats.

The Morning After

BREAKFAST BROWNIES AND CREAMY RASPBERRY COCOA

Breakfast brownies are a fun, mischievous choice for breakfast, served with cocoa and a fresh-picked flower or two to grace the bedside table.

RECIPES

Ginger Cake

1 package white cake mix
2 tsp candied ginger, finely chopped
1 tsp ginger powder

Prepare cake batter according to instructions, adding the ginger powder and candied ginger and stirring until well blended. Bake according to directions in a greased bundt cake pan. Invert onto a decorative cake plate and dust the top with powdered sugar. Serve with fresh whipped cream.

Shock Cocktails

In a metal mixing cup combine:
Ice
1 oz vodka
½ oz triple sec
½ oz lime juice

Shake and strain into two ice cold shot glasses.

If you top this shot with peach schnapps, it will become a tasty treat called a Meltdown. This drink is smoother going down. A trick for use with the Shock cocktail is to add either edible gold dust, or tiny shreds of 24k gold leafing to it right before pouring. Make sure that the gold has not been treated with any chemicals. Gold is completely digestible, but harsh chemicals are not. Some cinnamon schnapps manufacturers use the same technique. On a more serious note, you may try this passion-igniting little trick: A "Flaming Shock" can be made by carefully pouring 151 Rum into a teaspoon. Use a lighter to light fire to the rum in the teaspoon. Blow out the lighter. Carefully and slowly pour the flaming rum onto the surface of the cocktails. It will burn a pale, delicate flame for a few minutes. When you blow out the fire, wait several minutes before drinking the cocktail. The rim of the glass will be very hot. The best way to avoid waiting to drink your tasty cocktail is to shoot it quickly by pouring it into your mouth, never touching your lips to the glass.

I like to keep a beautiful, antique salt shaker of edible gold dust in the kitchen. It is perfect to dust on fine little pastries, to make whipped cream glittery, and to make cocktails just breathtaking.

Lively Lime Wine Seltzer (nonalcoholic)

Rub the rim of a wine glass in some corn syrup or honey with lime juice.

In a glass combine:

2 oz nonalcoholic white wine

Fill with lime soda

Garnish with three thin slices of lime.

Candied Lemon Rind

Rind of two lemons, white pith removed, and rind cut into thin strips

½ cup white sugar

½ cup water

Pour water and sugar into a microwave-safe bowl, stir once and add lemon peel. Microwave on high for 3 minutes. Remove, stir, and cook another 2 or so minutes until the liquid is syrupy. Drain off syrup and toss the peels with extra white sugar. When cool, store in an airtight container.

Breakfast Brownies

1 package white brownie mix

1 tsp vanilla extract

½ tsp ground cinnamon

1 egg

2 oz semisweet chocolate chips

Follow the directions on the package, and add the vanilla, cinnamon, and egg to the mixing bowl. Pour into a lightly greased baking pan. Melt the chocolate in a double boiler or a metal bowl placed over a small pot of simmering water. Drizzle the chocolate on top of the brownie mix, and bake. The additions will give the brownies more substance and give them a well-rounded flavor, which is perfect for the morning, and the perfect touch for your childish adventure—brownies for breakfast.

Creamy Raspberry Cocoa

Prepare instant hot cocoa according to the directions. Add 1 tsp raspberry syrup and 2 tsp instant powdered creamer. The syrup is commonly used for Italian soda and for flavoring snow cones. Top with whipped cream, and serve with a small bowl of fresh raspberries.

A Foreign Affair

Poem
"Speak to Me in Russian"

Activity
Strip Poker

Pulse Point Oil
Lilac

Color Scheme
Red Square Red

Menu
Pleasantly Pink Geranium Cake
and Almond Liqueur Soda or
Fresh Flower Water (nonalcoholic)

The Morning After
Buttered Toast with Orange-Vanilla Sugar,
Hot Cappuccino

Speak to Me in Russian

Whisper to me so softly that I can't hear, only see

your lips shape each word.

Make me imagine these words.

Make me believe each word means what I wish it would.

Speak to me in Russian.

Utter unfamiliar syllables that force me to swallow the urge to

kiss you as you speak,

interrupt you and tease your lips with mine.

Tell me something strange so that I may feel the power of the words

one at a time.

Then come closer, so slowly, and

breathe in time to the beating of my heart.

It beats so much faster as your mouth

comes nearer.

*T*his evening your date will feel weakened by desire for you, as every aspect of your time together has been carefully put together for total sensual appeal. The unfamiliar specialties you create will amaze both of you, and you will feel like breaking the cardinal rule: do not eat dessert first.

Setting the Scene

You should wear a tight, red sweater and a leather skirt or pants. The sheen of the leather will take the shock off the tightness of the sweater so your shape can be truly appreciated. Brown leather goes with absolutely everything, so buy a leather skirt or pants in a rich, chocolate brown. In any color, leather carries a tight, red sweater extremely well.

To make your home seem more authentically foreign, try not to use conventional lights. Use oil lamps instead, or many small, tallow-yellow candles.

Begin your date by window shopping together in town. Have an early dinner at a Russian, Mediterranean, Persian, or Indian restaurant in the afternoon. All of these choices go well with the evening you have planned. Retire to your place at sunset. Play some sorrowful violin music or a combination of strings. This music will create a mood all its own for your evening of new experiences. If you can find two tall, standing candleholders for the corners at the foot of the bed, one candle at each corner looks very nice. Also, you can make a permanent fixture by suspending two chains from the ceiling on hooks and fastening a wire cradle with a votive in it at the bottom of each one. You may be able to find some of these already made in specialty shops and bath stores.

Pulse Point Oil

Lilac

Lilac is very fragrant and most are not used to it. It smells like something that would have been used to make tiny, dark brown vials of perfume for exquisite women a hundred years ago. Your great grandmother would have treasured her dainty little foreign bottle of it, and she would have worn it whenever she went out with her favorite cameo pin on her chest. You will find fantasy in this fragrance as well. Dab it on each wrist and rub them together.

How to Serve the Poem

Compose your own poem, or use the one at the beginning of the chapter. Wait until after dinner as you are both coming through your front door. Stop in the dimly lit hallway. Bring your face close to his but do not kiss him. Recite the poem to him if you wish, or slip a card with the poem written on it into his hand. He will be unable to hold himself back from indulging in a long, soft kiss. Try a little Russian to heat things up. This is a short list of words that you can easily learn and use. It is not necessary to learn how to spell or write them.

"Hello, my love"—"Priviet, maya loobov"
"I love you"—"Ya tyebya loobloo"
"Kiss me"—"Potsoloy menya"

This is a crude lesson for a truly beautiful language. If you have an interest in learning this adorable way of communicating, buy a book of Russian for the beginner. It is fun to learn, and the two of you may find that you very much enjoy talking to each other this way. Learn nicknames for each other, and talk secretly in a crowd of people.

Menu
PLEASANTLY PINK GERANIUM CAKE AND ALMOND LIQUEUR SODA OR FRESH FLOWER WATER (NONALCOHOLIC)
The delectable cake should be started the day before as the fragrant flavors should be allowed to marry. The fragrance of the cake will be enhanced by the fragrance of the beverage, blending with the subtle scent of the pulse point oil. The sense of smell is one of the most powerful ways to a man's heart (and other parts, as well).

Activity
STRIP POKER
Strip poker is always a naughty way to interact with your date. A simple game of five-card draw is best. To play, draw five cards each, throw back from one to four cards, and pick an equal number of cards from the deck. You must now play the cards you have. The loser of each hand must relinquish an article of clothing. Of course, this game should be played by candlelight.

The Morning After
BUTTERED TOAST WITH ORANGE-VANILLA SUGAR, HOT CAPPUCCINO
Serve a light breakfast of buttered toast with orange-vanilla sugar in bed on a tray with a tiny vase holding a miniature red rose bud. Place several lace doilies on the tray and a napkin rolled up in a sterling silver ring. It can be a ring you purchased at a flea market for such a purpose, or a silver band that you would like to present as a gift to your man. Serve hot cappuccino with a kiss.

RECIPES

Pink Geranium Cake
There is almost no cake more wonderful or simple than this one. I use it often.

1 box of cake mix for plain, white cake
Culinary geranium leaves (from a good market, or grow your own from cuttings)
1 package of white frosting for one cake
red food coloring

Prepare the white cake batter according to the directions. Wash the geranium leaves, trim the stems off, and puncture the leaves as much as possible without shredding. Stir the leaves into the batter, add a few drops of the food coloring to make the batter pink, and let sit overnight in the fridge. The next day, remove all of the leaves and bake according to the directions. Let cool, then ice with the white frosting. Serve on small antique saucers.

ombine:

Noyeaux (pink almond liqueur)

Fresh Flower Water
To glasses of ice water, add a bunch of washed and trimmed pansies. The pansy is the most commonly used and the prettiest of all the edible flowers, but you can easily find others. Place a straw in each glass as well and a small tea light in a tiny dish next to each of your plates.

Edible flowers are not only for decoration in beverages, but can be enjoyed in any variety of foods. They can be brushed with egg whites and then coated with sugar to crystallize them for topping desserts; they can be frozen in ice cubes, tossed in salads, stirred into gelatin molds, even stuck into the tops of handmade candies and jellies.

Buttered Toast with Orange-Vanilla Sugar

1 oz orange powder
1 oz vanilla powder
1 oz white granulated sugar
4 slices white bread
4 pats butter

Purchase the flavored powders from a bakeshop that carries cake-decorating supplies. Mix the orange and vanilla powders with the sugar together in a small bowl and pour into an antique salt shaker to be used often. Toast two slices white toast, butter lightly, sprinkle with the orange-vanilla sugar.

Hot Cappuccino

Add one-half cup hot, fresh coffee to one-half cup fresh, steamed whole milk. You may want to purchase a cappuccino machine for this purpose, as the foam produced by the machine is wonderful. Sprinkle cinnamon or chocolate powder on top if you so desire.

The Next Exciting Step

Poem
"A Moment"

Activity
Firing Range

Pulse Point Oil
His Cologne

Color Scheme
White and Brown

Menu
White and Dark Chocolate Raspberries
and Sex on the Beach Cocktails or
Virgin Passion Cocktail (nonalcoholic)

The Morning After
Muffins and Mimosas or
Strawberry Lemonade (nonalcoholic)

A Moment

A moment is such a short time to enjoy eyes that are so beautiful,
and it's only a moment that we share.
Time enough for one thought when our eyes meet.
We rarely speak, we never touch, but each day we share a glance
and I anticipate it with pleasure and shyness.
Time slows in our moment.
I feel your touch across the space between us and
I spoon myself into your eyes.
I search them so that I may know what other colors and images
may be hiding, as long as our moment will allow.
And that I may know you only a little bit better.
I don't know how your hands touch, but I feel them,
and I don't know how hot our bodies would be when pressed together
but my skin feels flush with heat.
I ask your eyes what your lips would taste like,
and imagine your lips parting for me.
I ask would we kiss the same way,
and I pretend I can feel your warm hand on the back of my neck,
pulling me in to you for that kiss.
Time starts again.
Our moment passes.
You start to walk away.
My heart races,
and I'm left feeling a little bit naked
as you leave.

The act of firing a gun makes one feel very powerful, indeed. I recommend that all women try it at least once. The confidence you will feel will have a surprisingly erotic effect on your body. You may not notice it at first, but you definitely will afterward. Have a perfect dinner at a great French restaurant and drive around the scenic areas where you live. Do a little window shopping when it gets dark so you can gaze at the bright arrangements. Ask him about his likes and hopes. Spend time just listening to him. He will feel how interested you are in him. During the evening, send him subtle hints that you want to get intimate with him. After all, he can't read your mind. By touching his hand casually and letting your fingers stroke his skin just a little longer, he will know that you want to touch him more. A hand on the inside of his knee will show physical intentions without seeming overly aggressive. Touching his arm will make him feel strong and powerful, as will placing your hand on his chest. Avoid touching or stroking his face or shoulders as that will seem motherly or platonic and he may not realize that it is a sexual invitation. Also avoid really delicate areas such as his buttocks or hips, as that could seem too aggressive. Make sure that you make eye contact, and speak just a little slower and lower than usual. The pure sexiness of it will drive him crazy.

Setting the Scene

Buy a bouquet of filler foliage only; small, dry, pale flowers and ferns and such. It will not be as fresh as a full bouquet, but it will be very charming and easy on the eyes. It will also last a long time, and in a few small vases around your home will provide an intoxicating scent that he will find very alluring. An interesting choice is a few branches of coffee berries. Also, scatter a few berries, leaves, and small flowers around the base of the vase.

Pulse Point Oil

HIS COLOGNE

Find out what his favorite cologne is, and get a few samples of it at your local department store. You may find that it really works on your skin. He may love it on you as well. He will also know that you really pay attention to him. For this evening you can make a small candle in a tin or jar or glass with two teaspoons of his favorite cologne and make a gift of it. Beeswax beads can easily be melted down in a boil bag sold for the purpose. Many craft stores sell these implements as a kit. Add the fragrance right before pouring the wax. Wicks are very inexpensive and can be anchored with tape. Suspend the wick over the container by tying it to a pencil or drinking straw and placing the pencil on the rim. You can also make an extra one for yourself as a reminder of the evening. Surprise him by wearing some of the cologne yourself. You may discover that he likes it much better on you anyway.

To change his cologne into a cologne that you can easily wear, follow these simple steps. Use one ounce of cologne. Test the smell of the cologne first by spraying it on your wrist and letting it sit for five minutes. Smell your wrist. If it smells very woody, add ten drops of a fruity oil (peach, pear, or fig) and five drops of a floral oil (rose, lavender, or carnation). If the citrus scent is too strong, add seven or eight drops of frankincense, and a couple of drops of cucumber to lighten the fragrance. If it smells sharp and floral, add five drops grapefruit oil, five apple oil, and four violet or narcissus oil. Shake to mix; let sit overnight to marry the scents. Pour into your own bottle.

How to Serve the Poem

Compose your own poem, or use the one at the beginning of the chapter. Write the poem on a white, paper lace doily, which will be used for the white and dark raspberries. Write it the day before so that the ink won't run under the raspberries. He will start to notice it after a few berries. Ask him to read it out loud. Reading it will turn him on immensely, as it will you. His heart will race as he realizes what it means, and his nervousness will excite you as well. You both just want to please each other and this is your night to spend the entire time doing just that.

Menu

WHITE AND DARK CHOCOLATE RASPBERRIES AND SEX ON THE BEACH COCKTAILS OR VIRGIN PASSION COCKTAIL (NONALCOHOLIC)

You'll be serving sweet tart chocolate-dipped raspberries with a passion-packed cocktail. You may also wish to serve these luscious treats with tiny cordial glasses of Chambord, a fantastic deep purple liqueur of raspberries. If you can find white-chocolate-flavored liqueur (Godiva makes one; it's creamy white in color and delicious), combine the two in equal parts to make the creamiest, dreamiest dessert liqueur that you have ever tasted. Stir thoroughly in ice and strain before serving. Lick your lips.

Activity
Firing Range
All that you must do is find a shooting range nearby. Go to an indoor range only, as they have strict rules and take extra safety measures. When at the range, select a gun that fits comfortably in your hand. Purchase a target with a red bull's-eye as it will help you aim. Your date will most likely be very impressed by your skill. Simply aim slowly and take your time. You will probably surprise yourself. Take turns firing, and admire each other's form. Every few rounds, kiss (make sure you put down the guns first). Take the targets home to remind yourselves how powerful you are.

The Morning After
Muffins and Mimosas or Strawberry Lemonade (nonalcoholic)
Spend the morning talking about the firing range and taking another look at your targets. Remark upon each other's talents. Remembering how turned on you both became will awaken new passions.

RECIPES

White and Dark Raspberries

1 small package of fresh, ripe raspberries
¼ cup white chocolate chips
¼ cup dark chocolate chips

Melt each kind of chocolate separately in the microwave on high in 30 second bursts, or use the double boiler method, which takes longer but heats the chocolate more evenly. Either way, this dessert will come out perfectly.

When chocolate is melted and smooth, dip raspberries in it one by one and place on wax paper to harden. Dip all the raspberries and let sit at least one hour to cool.

When hard, remove from paper and pile into a crystal bowl, white on one side, and dark on the other. Garnish with a mint leaf.

Sex on the Beach Cocktails

In a large glass combine:
Ice
1 oz vodka
½ oz peach schnapps

Fill the rest of the glass with one-half orange juice and one-half cranberry juice. Pour into a serving glass. Garnish with a cherry.

Virgin Passion Cocktail

In a metal mixing cup combine:
1 oz sweet and sour mix
1 oz grenadine
3 oz passion fruit nectar

Shake and strain into a chilled cocktail glass. Garnish with a mint leaf.

Easy Muffins

For easy muffins, purchase a package of muffin mix and wake up early to bake them. With any mix you can add a cup of fresh berries or sliced bananas, whatever you choose. They will taste fresh and homemade even though they are not.

Mimosas

This is the easiest, and one of the best, beverages for morning (especially after an exciting night like the one you just had).

Chill tulip glasses in refrigerator overnight.
When ready to serve, dip the rim of the glass in powdered sugar.
Mix:
½ fresh orange juice
½ chilled champagne

Strawberry Lemonade

Combine one-half strawberry juice with one-half orange juice. Add a squeeze of lemon, lots of ice, a tall spoon, and a straw.

The Yearning Seduction

Poem
"The Hunter"

Activity
A Healthy Dose of Bondage

Pulse Point Oil
Fragrant Lemon Flower

Color Scheme
Black and Cream

Menu
Crab with Honey Butter, Fresh Frond
Salad, and Watermelon Champagne or
Virgin Pomegranate Punch

The Morning After
Strawberry Mimosas and a Friendly Game of Golf

The Hunter

A solemn, stern face that shows hunger and pride,
heightens my senses, and I need to hide.
In any small space that will offer some shade,
my capture is certain if slightly delayed.
For even at night you can feel where I'm crouched.
You pace around slowly and open your mouth,
to taste my direction and smell my tension,
and you're only delighted by my apprehension.
You patiently watch me until in my rage,
I leap from my shelter, my comforting cage.
You hold me to show your wiry strength,
and just for the pleasure of tightening your length.
To push inside deeper, sink into my hips, and
let the sweat cover and moisten your lips.
You look deeply at me and my worry has changed,
to wanting and needing, and passions enflamed.
Release me and again slowly, and keep teasing me,
'til I become frantic and pull you down to me.
Your hands hold my shoulders while my breath grows quick.
Your lips on my breast and our sweat becomes slick.
I cannot escape you, so lost I've become.
My body and yours have become only one.

"The Hunter" is how you say that you want to be captured. It is a tease, and an effective physical invitation. It shows your receptiveness to advances that have been made. This could also be your way of advancing first. This seduction is a game, and you are encouraged to play to your utmost. Do not be ashamed of your strong sexuality; it makes you the life-loving person you are, and he loves you for it. He may even be jealous of your passion for feeling things so deeply.

Setting the Scene

Dust a little bronzing powder in the crease of your cleavage and a tiny bit along the neck bone. Arrange a small vase with one or two deep red (almost black) tulips. The tulips will last for many days. Wear a tight ensemble of black and cream. White is usually too stark when next to black, but cream makes the outfit warmer and more approachable. Wear tight black slacks, a tight black top, and a long cream coat or cream blazer. Light a single candle by the bed and on the table. Dim the other lights almost all the way down. Try placing a magnifying glass in front of a candle. There are sconces and candleholders that are available this way, but it is easy enough to make one if you have the lens. The lens should be large and clean. Position it directly in front of the candle's flame. It makes a beautiful, deep light.

Pulse Point Oil

FRAGRANT LEMON FLOWER

Fragrant lemon flower is a lovely and lively combination for brightening up every day. Combine:

10 drops lemon oil

2 drops lemon verbena oil

4 drops freesia oil

2 drops rose oil

Add an equal amount of jojoba oil if using pure essential oils.

Pour into a tiny glass vial and let sit overnight to let the scents marry. Apply to pulse points. Make a simple sachet to freshen your lingerie cabinet by lightly scenting a cotton ball with the scent (preferably an oil-based scent) and placing in a tiny, sealed plastic bag dotted with little holes on the topside only. The scent will come out the top, and will not leak out the bottom. This scent in particular is great for the cabinet, and is fresh and pleasing without being too dominant.

How to Serve the Poem

Compose your own poem, or use the one at the beginning of the chapter. Write the poem on a small card in thick, black ink. Place the card in the top drawer of your lingerie cabinet, which is most likely the drawer you keep all of your tiny, delicate, hand-wash-only panties in. The sheer and otherwise sexy ones should be on top. While you are "freshening up," ask him to get a note pad out of the cabinet. He will find the poem and will read it in silence. In a moment, when you come out, you will find him panting and waiting for you. He will be unable to refrain from touching you all over. If you feel up to it, create special truffles for this seduction the day before. You can make a small gift box for him, as he will undoubtedly love them. Place his poem in the top of the box for him to take with him.

Menu

CRAB WITH HONEY BUTTER, FRESH FROND SALAD, AND WATERMELON CHAMPAGNE OR VIRGIN POMEGRANATE PUNCH

Tonight you'll want to dip the succulent crab into the honey butter and feed it to each other. Ooh la la!

Activity

A HEALTHY DOSE OF BONDAGE

Bondage doesn't always mean violence or pain. It can be quite the opposite. In the seduction, you are the master, and you are in control. You will be dressed in your most beguiling ensemble. Have soft music with a beat playing, something a bit techno is very appropriate. Undress him, lay him onto your bed, and tie his wrists to the bedposts with cut-off legs from a pair of black pantyhose. This material is soft, stretchy, and does not restrict movement. The "bondage" is symbolic. He will be your willing slave for the night. When you tell him to do something, or say something, he will. He will love every moment of this seduction. You may also tie his ankles together, and you may blindfold him. This will give you the freedom to do whatever you want to his body and the thrill of not being able to see you will drive him crazy. If you would like to change places with him, feel free.

The Morning After

STRAWBERRY MIMOSAS AND A FRIENDLY GAME OF GOLF

Make the strawberry mimosas ahead of time and pour them into a thermos to take with you. Go to a nearby golf course to enjoy some healthy gaming. Golf is a very difficult game to learn. Go to a beginner course and take your time. It is fun to learn, and even more fun to fail at. There are few things that can top whacking the ball farther than you can see. It will be great fun, and sporting together will bring you both closer. Rent a golf cart for the day. Walking with a bag of golf clubs is not easy. Even if you have never tried golf before, give it at least one day to charm you.

RECIPES

Crab with Honey Butter

1 lb crabmeat. Buy king crab legs if you can. They should be cooked but never frozen. Many markets will steam them for you. Crack the legs with a nutcracker, trying to keep the pieces whole.
½ cup butter, softened
¼ cup honey

Chill the crab meat in a bowl embedded in ice, or in a sculpted ice bowl. Whip the honey into the butter and continue to whip until fluffy. Pump the honey butter through a pastry tube onto a small plate. Make little starflowers on top of each other. Shaped tips make perfect little flower shapes. You could also try the ribbon attachment and make overlapping ribbons with the butter.

Fresh Frond Salad

Fronds are the unopened curls on a fern, which are also edible and are very delicious in salads. Ask a local gardener to provide you with some of the young plants. Make sure that they are the edible kind. I recommend using Ostrich Ferns for the best taste. Pluck the fronds and wash them. To grow your own, transfer them to a wooden planting box right outside of your kitchen. Pluck new fronds whenever you feel like an exotic salad.

Toss them with fresh spinach leaves, and splash them with a bottled raspberry vinaigrette. Top with a few raspberries.

Watermelon Champagne

In a chilled champagne flute combine:
1 oz watermelon schnapps
½ oz Crème de Noyeaux
Fill with chilled champagne

Garnish with a sugar coated strawberry, and rim the glass with lemon juice.

Virgin Pomegranate Punch

In a chilled tulip glass combine:

1 oz pomegranate juice (available at most Eastern food markets)

2 oz guava or pear nectar

Fill with lime soda

Garnish with a slice of pear or lime peel.

Strawberry Mimosas

In a chilled champagne flute combine:

½ chilled champagne

¼ fresh orange juice

¼ fresh strawberry nectar

Garnish with a strawberry slice and an orange slice.

For a nonalcoholic alternative, combine equal parts strawberry juice, orange juice, and pink lemonade for a sweet and refreshing punch—perfect for taking along with you.

The Messy Seduction

Poem
"Get Ready For Me"

Activity
Ice Cream and an Action Flick

Pulse Point Oil
Lavender Lime

Color Scheme
Cream and Lavender

Menu
Banana Splits and Amaretto Shake
or Ice-Cold Milk

The Morning After
Banana Nut Muffins with Maple Butter
and Café au Lait

Get Ready for Me

Hold me:

until my hands roam your body

and rub every inch of skin and muscle.

Kiss me:

when my lips start to tremble and you can feel the heat pumping, til you can

see its strength in the center of my eyes.

Stroke the thin lace of my panty with one finger, gently.

Touch me:

when I kiss you harder with every moment and

I lick your skin with a hungry tongue.

Lower me:

to the ground when your body screams for me and

I tell you to take me through the lace, and when the

sweat beads on your back and chest and makes us slippery.

Finally enter me:

when the wetness makes you whisper one raspy word, "Yes," and

then push so hard that you tear through the lace and

make me gasp.

Setting the Scene

Have dinner out together at a new restaurant that neither of you have tried before. An expensive restaurant is the best way to light erotic fires. Make yourself absolutely lovely in a short skirt and becoming top. Before you go out, arrange your kitchen in an inviting way with all of the ingredients laid out on the counter in the order in which they will be needed. This will help you and your date jump right into the task at hand when you get back.

Pulse Point Oil

LAVENDER LIME

Dab a tiny bit of a mixture of lavender and lime oils onto your pulse points. If the oil is pure, dilute it with jojoba oil, as always. Dab a little of it on a curtain. The scent will drift toward you throughout the evening. Lavender is quite pungent, so use it sparingly.

How to Serve the Poem

Compose your own poem, or use the one at the beginning of the chapter. Handwrite the poem on an old card made of antique parchment. It is always a good idea to get antique stationary every chance you get as you never know when you may feel an urge to get artistic and use some naughty calligraphy. Place the poem on your bed pillow with a mint chocolate on top.

Menu

BANANA SPLITS AND AMARETTO SHAKE OR ICE-COLD MILK

Make the dessert together and sweet things will follow.

Activity

ICE CREAM AND AN ACTION FLICK

As soon as you get back to your place, invite him into the kitchen to help you make the banana splits. While this is in progress, bend over to pick something up a couple of times and make sure he notices. He should get a little something on him, preferably in a place where you can lick it off of him. Have a movie set up which is full of gratuitous explosions and such. He will absolutely love it, and most women love these movies as well, as they are always full of unnecessary machismo and half-naked men. When you sit down to your movie, have the lights low so that accidents will happen with the ice cream. Eat out of the same bowl and share one spoon. He should be the one feeding you. If you happen to get a little on your chest or inner thigh, well, you get the idea.

The Morning After
BANANA NUT MUFFINS WITH MAPLE BUTTER AND CAFÉ AU LAIT

Wake early to prepare the muffins. The fresher these are, the better they taste, and there is nothing like melting butter on a warm muffin right out of the oven. Take your time eating together. Have the meal by a sun-dappled window, or outside if you can. Think of wonderful relaxing things that you can do together today. You could go swimming, go window shopping in a new part of town, or go to a flea market and look for hand-blown glass. You can do anything. This day is for the two of you. Do not waste a moment of precious time together.

RECIPES

Banana Splits

2 whole bananas
chocolate, vanilla, and strawberry ice creams
whipped cream
chocolate sauce
caramel sauce
chopped nuts
candy sprinkles

Cut the bananas in half and place them in two ice cream dishes. Place a scoop of each kind of ice cream on top. Top off with chocolate sauce, then caramel sauce, followed by whipped cream, nuts, and sprinkles.

Amaretto Shake

In a blender combine:
A handful of ice
½ cup whole milk
1 oz amaretto
1 oz chocolate sauce

Blend until smooth.

Banana Nut Muffins

1 package of muffin mix
1 cup mashed, ripe bananas
½ cup chopped walnuts

Prepare the muffin batter according to directions, adding the bananas and nuts. Pour into muffin tins and bake according to directions.

Maple Butter

¼ lb butter, softened
¼ cup maple syrup
½ tsp cinnamon

Microwave the butter for 20 seconds or until liquefied. Whip together all ingredients with an electric blender and pour into an attractive container from which the butter will be served to accompany the muffins.

Café au Lait

If you use a percolator, use as much grounds as you would for a normal pot, but only use half as much water. Then add hot milk to two ounces of strong coffee.

The Unforgettable Seduction

Poem
"I Really Love Where This Is Going"

Activity
Butterscotch Sauce Body Painting,
Apricot-Vanilla Shower

Pulse Point Oil
Peach and Anisette

Color Scheme
Cream and White

Menu
Dine Out on Steak, Tiramisu, and
Pink Squirrel Cocktail or
Virgin Amaretto Sour

The Morning After
Traditional Dutch Coffee

I Really Love Where This Is Going

I take in the sensations you give me like a new language,

not like any I've heard or studied.

Movement and sounds, smells, and the electricity in your fingers

moving from one part of me to another.

I can't close my eyes,

watching you move toward me and into me is teaching me more.

My chest pounds to the rhythms going through me,

like sounding the syllables of your passion language.

I translate that you want me, like the taste of me,

that you like the sound of my moans, loud or soft,

and that you need my hands on your sides, urging you to me.

We repeat the words of the language together,

whispering to each other, close and deep.

We understand what they mean to us only.

Finally we begin to breathe together,

and we know perfect comprehension of this language.

The language that we created,

and learned,

and speak.

*T*his seduction is for those who like what they've been seeing and getting and want to get some more. It is simple and direct. Its meaning cannot possibly be mistaken. You tell him about every physical intention you have for him. His body will respond in ways it never has before. You have gotten to know each other and you understand each other's needs and ideals. Now you will proceed.

Setting the Scene

Make your bed with clean sheets that you aren't that attached to, as the butterscotch will make quite a mess. Take the comforters and blankets off of the bed and remove any decorative pillows. Use an old blanket, but make sure it smells lovely. Have clean sheets ready to put on the bed later. You do not want to sleep in butterscotch no matter how much you like it.

Have the bed turned down and two small plates of tiramisu waiting on a tray on the night table. Have pink squirrels or virgin amaretto sours waiting in the refrigerator, and the butterscotch in a small crystal jar with two brand-new, good-quality paint brushes at bedside as only the good ones will keep all of their bristles.

Pulse Point Oil

PEACH AND ANISETTE

To create this absolutely fabulous combination of scents, mix five drops of peach oil with one drop of anisette oil. Add jojoba and dot behind your knees and on your wrists. The mixture of the fresh peach and the exotic anisette will entice your date as it seduces your sense of smell. You may very well turn yourself on with this scent.

How to Serve the Poem

Compose your own poem, or use the one at the beginning of the chapter. Give this poem to him at dinner when you are finishing your meal. Write it with a good black pen onto a gorgeous swatch of fabric with frayed edges. You can fray the edges yourself by scraping a fork over the edges for a few minutes. Dab the swatch with a bit of your favorite perfume. Once the ink is completely dry, usually within a few hours, spray the swatch with a bit of hairspray from twelve inches away. This will help stiffen the fabric and better the effect.

Menu

DINE OUT ON STEAK, TIRAMISU, AND PINK SQUIRREL COCKTAILS OR VIRGIN AMARETTO SOUR (NONALCOHOLIC)

Enjoy a great steak at a well-known steakhouse; try the steak rare, and with a dish of fresh Béarnaise sauce on the side to accompany the meat. A single glass of dry red wine will make the flavor of the meat rich and buttery in your mouth. Chew slowly and enjoy every moment of your time together. After you have enjoyed your romantic evening out together, you will arrive back at your place with the sumptuous tiramisu waiting. The creamy consistency of the dessert is soothing to the tongue, and the pink squirrel cocktails are exciting without over-powering you. The virgin amaretto sours are fabulous and exotic.

Activity

BUTTERSCOTCH SAUCE BODY PAINTING, APRICOT-VANILLA SHOWER

Begin by removing all of your clothing (keep your underwear on if you are self-conscious and don't mind getting it sticky). Sit on the bed facing each other, cross-legged with your knees touching and the butterscotch sauce between you. Take turns making strokes with the brushes dripping with sweet, sticky sauce, painting where you wish. Give attention to whatever lines and shapes you like, as he does the same. You may discover new favorite spots on each other. When you make a mistake, lick the sauce off and start over. When you have used up the sauce, or have reached your boiling point, put the jar and brushes aside and do what comes natu-rally. Afterwards, shower off using the apricot-vanilla shower gel and a loofah. Have large fluffy towels or robes to wrap each other in.

Butterscotch Sauce

1 cup dark corn syrup
1 cup sugar
½ cup half-and-half
2 tbsp butter
Pinch of salt
1 tsp vanilla

Combine all ingredients in a saucepan except vanilla and cook over medium heat stirring constantly, until the mixture comes to a full, rolling boil. Boil briskly for five minutes, stirring occasionally. Remove from heat. Add the vanilla and serve warm.

You can purchase gold dust from a fine bakery and add a little to the sauce. It will add a nice bit of glitter.

This sauce can be enjoyed on ice cream, cakes, over coffee topped with whip cream, or, like tonight, drizzled on each other. This, of course, is the ultimate dessert. You can make the butterscotch up to two weeks ahead of time and store it in the fridge. Enjoy a steamy apricot-vanilla shower afterward and you will have sweet, sweet dreams in each other's arms.

Apricot-Vanilla Shower Gel

This shower gel will be the most delicious bath fragrance you may ever have encountered, and you will want to have some handy at all times. Have large, fluffy towels or robes to wrap each other in. Follow the shower with full body kisses that will taste wonderful.

1 cup unscented shower gel or unscented baby shampoo
2 tsp each vanilla and apricot fragrance oils

Stir oils into shower gel completely, stirring slowly. Pour into a pretty glass pump bottle. If you live with your dream date, it is an intimate experience for you to make a morning routine of it. Feed each other a quick breakfast, smile over coffee, and suds each other up every day. This delicious gel keeps for six months. Store excess gel in a cool place.

The Morning After
TRADITIONAL DUTCH COFFEE

Enjoy early morning light with dutch coffee and whatever pastry you desire. Have a fresh flower in a tiny vase. Perhaps you will be in the mood to visit an arboretum or other museum. If there is an exciting traveling exhibition on display in your area, this is the perfect way for you to spend your day together.

RECIPES

Tiramisu

Ladyfingers (recipe to follow, or 1 box of store-bought ones)
½ cup heavy cream
1 16-oz container ricotta cheese
½ cup plus 2 tbsp sugar
8 oz semisweet chocolate chips
1 ½ cups strong coffee
unsweetened cocoa powder

Chill a medium bowl in the freezer. In another bowl, combine the ricotta cheese and ½ cup of the sugar. Remove the bowl from the freezer and pour the cream into it. Beat the cream with an electric mixer at high speed until it forms stiff peaks. Fold the whipped cream into the ricotta mixture with a rubber spatula, then add the chocolate chips.

Line the bottom of a medium-sized glass serving bowl with half of the ladyfingers. Stir the last two tablespoons of sugar into the coffee. Spoon the coffee over the ladyfingers until they are soaked through. Spread one-fourth of the cheese mixture over the cookies and add another layer of cookies. Soak the cookies with coffee, layer on the cheese, and so on until you have four layers of each, ending with a ricotta cheese layer.

Cover and refrigerate four hours. Sprinkle with cocoa powder just before serving. For an exquisite touch, place a paper lace doily lightly on the top of the tiramisu and then dust with cocoa powder. Carefully lift the doily and you will have a beautifully decorated cake.

Ladyfingers

3 egg whites
pinch of salt
⅓ cup sugar
3 egg yolks
1 tsp vanilla
⅔ cup sifted cake flour

Heat oven to 375° F. Grease and flour a large cookie sheet. Beat egg whites until soft peaks form. Add sugar gradually and beat well after each addition. Beat eggs until stiff and glossy. Beat the egg yolks and vanilla until thick and lemon colored. Quickly and gently fold in egg whites. Fold in the flour. Press through a pastry tube using a large, plain tip. Squeeze two-and-one-half inch strips onto a cookie sheet. If you do not have a pastry tube, fill a freezer bag with the dough and snip a corner of the bag with scissors and squeeze out the strips that way. Bake 8 to 10 minutes, or until set and very lightly browned on the bottom. Remove from the cookie sheet and cool on a rack. Store in a tightly closed box.

It is always a great idea to have ladyfingers on hand to enjoy with coffee, so certainly save some for the following morning to be served with the Irish coffee.

Pink Squirrel Cocktails
Chill two cocktail glasses.
In a metal mixing cup, combine:
Ice
1 oz White Creme de Cocoa
1 oz Crème de Noyeaux
4 oz cream

Shake and strain into the two chilled cocktail glasses. This recipe is already doubled. You can make four drinks ahead of time, and pour them into a crystal decanter to have at your bedside. You may also want to use sturdy glasses so that you will not spill them.

Virgin Amaretto Sours
Chill two cocktail glasses.
In a metal mixing cup, combine:
Ice
½ oz almond syrup
3 oz orange juice
dash of grenadine for color

Shake and strain into a glass, and garnish with an orange twist or candied orange peel (available at any fine chocolate boutique).

Traditional Dutch Coffee

In a coffee mug combine:

1 sugar cube, white or brown

1 oz chocolate syrup

hot fresh coffee

1 broken cardamon seed. (These are available at any supermarket in the spice aisle. They are large seeds that pack a lot of punch. The flavor is intense. To use them in coffee and in other foods, bite into a seed to release the flavor and let it soak in the coffee or sauce for a few minutes)

Let sit for a few minutes, stir, then serve.

Look at Me Like That Again

Poem
"I Like How You've Been Looking at Me"

Activity
Paddle Boating Turned Skinny-dipping

Pulse Point Oil
Sweet and Easy Berry

Color Scheme
Peaches and Creams

Menu
Clam Chowder and
White Wine or White Grape
Spritzer (nonalcoholic)

The Morning After
Mint Muffins and Hot Tea

I Like How You've Been Looking at Me

Are we wrong for each other?

Speechless are we when we meet.

Petty greetings are our masks.

We chat briefly and we're shallow but still can we see each other underneath.

We're intuitive and full of passion.

I consider that you feel nothing when you look at me, and

that you think I return in coldness.

Who do you want?

Is it me?

I see you and think, yes!

Who is the other who looks at you with the same need?

I'm happy with the way things are.

My heart caught in my throat tells me that I lie.

Would I change things?

When we meet I can see my body lie with yours,

To kiss you, touch your face, and

see all of you.

Who do you want?

I'll tell you the romance with my eyes when I meet you again tomorrow.

Tell me then.

Who do you want?

Hear my thoughts whisper to you of my love and

tell me then.

Who do you want?

"I Like How You've Been Looking at Me" is a soul-baring poem that is sure to endear. He will be very interested in learning more about you—as much as he can. Who is this sexy poet? Why has she chosen me? Make sure he is worthy of your attentions, as he must earn your favor and love.

Do not be afraid to show a man that you can cook. It is the way to his heart. Anyone will agree. When we feel hungry, we feel hollow, and a warm, perfectly flavored meal fills us with joy. You are not matronly, and you are not domestic. You are free, untamable, and on top of it all you know how to cook. That makes you perfect.

Setting the Scene

Use handfuls of fresh rose petals as potpourri and place a few in your lingerie drawers just for you. A bowl full of petals by your bed is ten times as feminine as dried potpourri. To get the most fragrance out of the petals, pierce some with your fingernails. Place a small bowl of the petals under the light of a table lamp to let the heat release the fragrance from them. Arrange eclectic bowls on the table for the chowder. Place a small vase on the table with daisies, a very friendly flower with a delightfully clean smell.

Pulse Point Oil

SWEET AND EASY BERRY

To create sweet and easy berry, combine two drops each of peach, rose, cherry, cucumber, and tulip oil. Add an equal amount of jojoba oil. Let sit overnight to allow the scents to marry. Dab onto pulse points. This is a great oil to add to a steamy bath for one. Indulge yourself.

How to Serve the Poem

Compose your own poem, or use the one at the beginning of the chapter. Write the poem on a thin piece of paper and roll it into a scroll. Tie with raffia and a knot. Put the tube into a tiny bottle if you are feeling cute. Give this to him as he is leaving and tell him to read it when he gets home. He will want to call you immediately after reading it to express his utter joy. It will be kept in his nightstand drawer for frequent reading.

Menu
CLAM CHOWDER AND WHITE WINE OR WHITE GRAPE SPRITZER

After the paddle boating, etc., retire to your place to rest and indulge in some sinfully rich and dreamy clam chowder. The creamy soup and pert beverage will soothe both of you into a lazy, blissful state.

Activity
PADDLE BOATING TURNED SKINNY-DIPPING

Start this seduction on a weekend morning—Saturday is best. Go paddle boating today. If the water is warm, have a swim and enjoy being a fish. Don't tell him, but remove your suit and place it inside the paddleboat. He will notice soon enough. There is nothing wrong with being naked (unless it is illegal in your area); you are just being yourself. Make sure you are parked nearby, and bring a robe to put on in a hurry if necessary. Otherwise, relax. Skinny-dipping is primal, and will let him know that nothing scares you. You will feel like an Amazon woman forever afterward.

The Morning After
MINT MUFFINS AND HOT TEA

If you feel like continuing the nudity trend, enjoy breakfast in the nude, or with only a thin sheet around you. Indulge in some quiet, naked sunbathing by a window or simply go outside if your yard is private.

RECIPES

Clam Chowder

Clams are an aphrodisiac, so use fresh clams if you can. If not, the difference in taste is slight. Use an extra amount of clams in the chowder if both of you favor them. Make this chowder in the morning before the date, and then you will only need to heat it up.

2 5-oz cans whole baby clams, liquid reserved. Use fresh clams if you can, and be sure to wash them thoroughly
4 slices of honey flavored ham, cut into small squares
½ onion, finely chopped
1 cup water (including clam liquid)
1 small potato, peeled and diced
½ tsp salt
¼ cup butter, softened
Pinch of pepper
1 ½ cups milk

Remove the clams from the liquid. In a soup pot combine ham and onion, and cook a few minutes. Measure clam liquid and add enough water to make one whole cup of liquid. Add this to the ham and onion mixture along with potatoes, salt, and pepper. Cover and cook over medium-low heat for fifteen minutes until potatoes are tender. Add milk and clams and bring just about to a boil, stirring constantly. Do not boil. Stir in butter. Serve immediately with a dry, white wine or white grape spritzer with a loaf of crusty bread.

White Grape Spritzer

In a glass carafe combine:
½ white grape juice and ½ seltzer water
A handful of washed, halved white grapes

Serve the carafe at tableside and drink out of wine glasses.

Mint Muffins

Nothing could be easier. For the mint muffins, use a package of plain muffin mix. Mix the batter according to directions, add many pierced mint leaves, stir, and refrigerate. Let sit overnight. The next day, remove the leaves and bake according to directions.

Tea

Always use a ceramic pot for serving tea. Warm the pot by holding it under hot water first. Pour boiling water into the pot containing one teabag per six ounces of water plus "one for the pot." If using loose tea, add one teaspoon of loose leaves plus one more "for the pot." Let the tea steep for five minutes and stir before pouring. I always like to use cubes of brown sugar and a slice of lemon. Garnish the tea saucer with a rose petal, and toss a couple of pierced rose petals into the teapot. It will add a touch of rose flavor.

Again, and Again

Poem
"Do It Again"

Activity
Honey Dust Feather Treatment

Pulse Point Oil
Orange Blossom

Color Scheme
Burnt Orange and Buttery Yellow

Menu
Oyster Appetizers and
Black Vodka Teasers or
Forbidden Virgin Punch

The Morning After
Crêpes à l'Orange, Orange Mint Tea,
and a Spa Day Trip

Do It Again

Your image glows in my mind and my lips tremble in memory as the

light touch of your kiss on bare skin lingers.

Alone at night, I relive every meeting, in the light, in the dark,

in a crowd of people whose faces have no meaning.

I run my lips over the back of my hand.

You first touched me there, and

I feel every caress, whether gentle or firm,

repeat and again.

Your face is etched into daydreams and

as my eyes close,

you watch with an intensity that makes me want you.

Dark eyes that hold such secrets and fire that they make mine alight.

As my room shrouds itself in a dark blanket,

I search for you, once again, before me,

in the blackness that is your only clothing.

"Do It Again" is a sexy way to bring up something intimate that you've done together. Do something nice for yourself, something that you maybe haven't considered a necessary expense before, such as getting an expensive French manicure, or having your hair colored. You want him to be surprised, and to feel that you made the effort for him. Make yourself feel even more special by buying the perfect shoes to go with your best outfit for this seduction. They could be fuzzy bedroom slippers with a stiletto heel—whatever makes you happy.

Setting the Scene

Plan this seduction for an early Friday evening. Arrange your table with a dark orange table-cloth and matching cloth napkins. Place one large, dark yellow candle in the center of the table in a crystal bowl to catch and reflect the light.

Pulse Point Oil

ORANGE BLOSSOM

Only use a tiny bit of the orange blossom oil on your pulse points; it is very pungent, and although orange blossoms do not smell like orange, it is quite a lovely scent. The subtlety of the fragrance when worn lightly adds to the mixed aromas of the meal, and it interacts with the exotic fragrance of the oysters. It is a favorite of Asian women, and is used in many of the more erotic perfumes on the market today. I often use this oil to layer under musky commercial blends.

How to Serve the Poem

Compose your own poem, or use the one at the beginning of the chapter. Write this poem on a small card hidden inside a gift package of fine truffles or a bouquet. Glue a small magnet to the back of the card. He will no doubt put it on his refrigerator or somewhere on his bath-room mirror to remind him of you, always; and it will give him sweet, sweet memories. Dab a bit of the orange blossom oil on the back of the card as well.

Menu

OYSTER APPETIZERS AND BLACK VODKA TEASERS OR FORBIDDEN VIRGIN PUNCH

These oysters should slip easily into your mouth and be chewed only lightly before swallowing. Oysters are among the most sensual foods, and tonight is a night for pure sensuality.

Activity
Honey Dust Feather Treatment

Honey dust is available at most adult shops. Do not be shy about entering one of these shops. Everyone else is trying to avoid eye contact as well, and will never notice you. If the shop does not have a large feather to go with it, you can purchase one at a craft store or at a silk floral shop. The honey dust feather treatment is the perfect way to get to know each other's sweet and ticklish spots. Lay a soft, washable blanket down on the floor in the living room and light many candles; small, yellow candles will glow well in the light. Place the candles around the entire perimeter of the blanket. It will seem as though it is forbidden to leave the confines of the blanketed area. This is what you want, as he should not be allowed to move from the blanket until you have had your fill of him. Start with just the obvious spots, then begin to discover new and unknown areas such as the back of his neck, in the crook of your elbow, the inside of his thigh, your cheek, and around the curve of your jaw. Dust each other lightly with the dust and proceed to lick it off. It has a light, sweet flavor and will add spark to many an evening. The dust will catch in the flames but will not ignite; it will simply make the air more enchanting as it fills the room with the faint smell of burnt honey.

The Morning After
Crêpes à l'Orange, Orange Mint Tea, and a Spa Day Trip

Wake earlier to prepare this light breakfast and enjoy breakfast in bed together, as you will want to get an early start. Find a spa in your area (where you can go as a couple) that has all the amenities; hot tubs, mud baths, mineral baths, a great bar and restaurant, and clear pools. Bring your most flattering swimsuit, or buy a new one that shows every curve at its voluptuous best. You will drive so he can rest his head on your shoulder and share his thoughts on the way there.

RECIPES

Oyster Appetizers

Have a good vendor shuck eight or ten live oysters in front of you to guarantee freshness. You can leave the oysters uncooked in this recipe, but steam them if you have not yet developed a taste for these slippery, wet, little things. Wash and then steam the oysters six or seven minutes, covered, in a small saucepan in one-half inch of water on high heat. Remove and let cool. Remove them from their shells and replace. This is to make sure that they will slip easily into your eager mouths.

Combine in a small bowl:
1 tbsp butter
1 tsp Tabasco
Large pinch horseradish
1 tsp soy sauce
½ tsp salt
½ tsp pepper
1 tsp lemon juice

Heat in the microwave just until melted, about one minute, and then pour into the shells over the oysters, filling the shells. Let cool, then sprinkle with finely diced, seeded tomatoes. You can always add an extra splash of lemon juice right before serving and more Tabasco if you prefer tangier foods.

Black Vodka Teasers

In a pretty decanter combine:
6 oz fine vodka
3 oz sweet and sour mix
3 oz sweetened lime juice
Black food coloring (available in craft stores and bakery supply shops)

This vodka should be very dark green or black from the addition of the coloring. The food coloring will not hurt you and will not dye your tongue. This is a very strong, very sour drink. Enjoy it ice cold in small, crystal shot glasses with the oysters.

Forbidden Virgin Punch

In a tumbler combine:

1 oz guava nectar

1 oz orange juice

1 tsp honey

Fill with cream soda

Garnish with a red licorice vine (this can also be used as a straw).

Crêpes à l'Orange

These are so easy to make that you could make them every morning for breakfast. You could also try them frozen. You may wish to prepare the crepes the day before. This will keep the morning simple, and you will have more time to languish in bed.

2 eggs

1 tsp sugar

½ tsp salt

½ cup flour

1 ⅓ cups milk

2 tbsp melted butter

In a bowl, beat the eggs until light. Add sugar and salt, beating constantly. Add flour, milk, and melted butter alternately, still beating. Batter will be very thin. Cook the pancakes on a lightly greased pan with a six-inch base. Pour a scant one-fourth cup of batter at a time. Swirl around the pan to spread as thin as possible. Brown on the first side, and turn carefully to bake the other side. Place between paper towels and keep separated until all crepes are done.

Orange Sauce

½ cup soft butter

1 cup sugar

½ cup orange juice

1 egg, well beaten

Grated rind from 1 orange

1 can whipped cream (for filling)

Combine all ingredients except whipped cream in a saucepan. Cook over medium heat until barely boiling, stirring constantly. Fill the crepes with whipped cream, roll up, place on a plate, and top with the orange sauce.

Orange-Mint Tea

In a small ceramic pot, place two tea bags of mint tea and two tea bags of orange tea, fill with hot water, and let steep five minutes. Serve in tiny teacups with a thin slice of lemon and one brown sugar cube.

Part Three

Essentials for Every Woman

Dressing for Every Passion

Your outfit for the evening will say the most about you before you even open your mouth; keep it simple. The most erotic colors have always been black, maroon, deep purple, forest green, navy blue, and dark red. If you have a favorite yellow dress, then by all means wear it, but colors communicate feelings, and you do not want to have to compete with your outfit for attention.

Color can change your moods like day and night. A color can cheer you up when you are depressed as easily as it can turn a great mood into a bad one. Try to choose the best colors for yourself everyday. You may notice major differences in how you feel and react to others, and how they react to you.

Clothing in any combination can be acceptable if you like it, just bear in mind that warm colors match well with other warm colors, as do cool colors with cool. But warm and cool colors never mix well with each other. Try not to wear black on black unless it's black pantyhose with a black skirt, or a black bra and black panties, as subtle color differences will be noticeable.

If you are carrying a favorite outfit from day into night, you may only need to change your shoes. Wear strappy stilettos with a great business suit and a fantastic purse, or change from pumps to boots with a prim skirt and cardi

Use this handy color chart every day, and always follow your mood.

COLOR	PROS	CONS	NOTES
Black	You will feel intelligent and dominant. Wear black when you need to be taken very seriously.	You might lose confidence and sensitivity. People will not be open to you and vice versa.	Black goes well with any color except for black. Mix it up, and put the color where you want to attract attention.
Brown	You will feel sincere and trustworthy. People will see you as a well-centered person.	You may be shy and unwilling to flirt. People may not be immediately drawn to you.	Brown always goes very well with black and neutrals.

COLOR	PROS	CONS	NOTES
White	You will feel lighthearted, fresh, and inspiring. People will see you as spirited.	You may feel alone or lonely. People may not feel at ease when approaching you.	White goes well with any color except black, as the contrast is often too stark. Mix neutrals such as tans, beiges, and browns with white for a classy effect.
Blue	You will be very sensitive and intuitive. You will be approached by many.	You may be oversensitive to the ills of others. Wearing blue can make you blue.	Wear any color shoes with a blue suit, but do not wear blue shoes. Try tans, maroons, and grays.
Purple	You will be open, creative, and willing. People will have immediate admiration for you.	It may make you rude, impatient, and irritating. People will then find you arrogant.	Beige and pale yellow anything looks fabulous with purple, especially if the purple is leather.
Red	You will feel as if you can take on the world. People will see you as a leader and a strong woman.	You could be quick tempered and impulsive. You may seem greedy and tense.	Wear an understated piece with the red item to mellow the brightness. If you are wearing a red suit, more power to you.
Orange	You will be creative, practical, and talkative. You will be a good decision-maker.	You might be confused and restless. People could feel that you are very competitive.	A pair of orange leather jeans instantly make me feel great. Try the color, but make it count.
Green	You will be clever and perceptive. People will see you as the "idea" person.	You could be untrusting and suspicious of those around you. People may see you as dishonest and tricky.	Emerald suits make people green with envy. Get a tight one. Also, try to wear understated colors with the green item.
Yellow	You will be deep and interesting. People will want to do things with you.	You could feel insecure and worried. Others may depress you.	Wear naturals, creams, beiges, and browns with yellow to pull off a very classy look.

Bath Temperature Guide

Baths are used for many purposes—to relax, heal, energize, etc. The temperature and length of the bath is what determines the effect the bath will have on you.

Stimulating Bath

For a stimulating bath, use only warm water, not hot, and don't let the bath go longer than fifteen minutes. Bergamot is a good oil to add for this bath, or add a half-teaspoon of synthetic vanilla extract. Place a live plant in a pot near the tub to create a peaceful environment and to add a little extra oxygen. Mix any essential oil into turkey red oil so as not to leave an oily ring around the tub. You may want to toss in some fresh mint leaves from your garden (I keep some growing in a small pot on the kitchen windowsill) for an especially stimulating bath.

Relaxing Bath

For a relaxing bath, use very hot water and let the bath run long, about thirty minutes. You'll start to feel drowsy and your cares will melt away. Use a couple of drops of sandalwood and orange essential oil, and a few rose petals or other fresh flowers. Bring a warm cup of lemon tea into the bath with you, or, if you have had an especially bad day, try bringing a cocktail or a Mexican coffee with a cinnamon stick. Try not to eat anything right before you go to sleep, as it will keep you awake.

Soothing Bath

For a soothing bath to ease the pain of sore muscles and overworked limbs, draw warm to hot water and let the bath run about twenty minutes. Eucalyptus is great for this bath, but may be a bit strong; add more water to the tub to lessen the scent slightly. Soften the eucalyptus with some lavender and add two to three drops of orange food coloring to the water. Some bath stores also carry specially formulated coloring drops for the tub. If a very soft scent is what you seek, try peach oil lightened with a drop or two of amber or vanilla.

Exhilarating Bath

For an exhilarating bath, let the water run just a bit cooler than you would really like and only stay in for five to seven minutes. Add a little scoop of Epsom salt and a couple drops of lemon verbena or mint oil to the water. Adding a bit of seaweed to the water and a bit of extra salt will excite your spirit as well as your body and bring you back to nature. You will feel just like a supple mermaid. The salts are also great for exfoliating dead skin. Scrub a small handful of salt into your rough spots such as the soles of your feet, knees, and elbows. Avoid broken skin.

The Bathroom

You never know when you may have a bathing partner and you don't want to have to think of scrubbing the tub. Have an upper shelf in the shower for all those bottles and gadgets so that they never get in your way. Keep candles in your bathroom as well, and burn anytime, especially while treating yourself to a therapeutic bath with essential oils. Most essential oils leave a greasy ring in the tub. However, using red turkey oil as a base for all of your bath oils greatly reduces this problem. Keep the bathroom pristine by using an after-shower spray cleaner every day.

A drop or two of essential oil in the top of the candle you are burning, or on a lightbulb in the bathroom will add a wonderful fragrance that will last a long time. Always keep at least a few fresh flowers on the counter for your own enjoyment, or some freshly plucked petals in a bowl to scatter in the bath water. The petals can reflect your mood. Use daisy petals if you're feeling light and carefree. Use foxgloves and a few leaves if you're feeling mysterious and naughty. Use sweetly colored rose petals if you are feeling romantic. Use any combination of petals and express yourself in creating your own mood.

Buy yourself a bouquet of flowers every once in a while. Place it in the bathroom where you will see it every time you look in the mirror.

Plants in the bathroom are essential as they promote calm, are beautiful when covered with mist after a shower, and provide extra oxygen. Ferns and similar plants do very well with the damp environment. Hanging one or two from the ceiling by a mirror will give the appearance of twice as many plants. I like to have a small wispy fern in the corner over the shower. With enough plants in the bathroom, you can feel as if you are showering in a rain forest.

Decorating your bathroom should be easy and fun. Use whimsical items like seashells. Hang some of your own artwork on the walls (frame them, of course, if they are special to you). Use a sea sponge to create a new paint treatment on the walls, or paint the trim of the door and windows a contrasting or dark color that you like. A very sensual color combination to try is a matte grapefruit on the walls with a deep maroon high-gloss for the trim, door, and window frames. Leaf through decorator's magazines to find the looks that you like the best and try them. You may really like the way the mirror looks with little painted vines growing on it.

Exciting Little Extras
Napkin Folding

Cloth napkins can be prefolded and stored in the pantry until you need them. It is amazing how much class and beauty they bring to the table. You may never want to be without them. Creating a folded napkin with a cute pocket for items such as silverware, breadsticks, a flower, a cookie, or your poem, is useful for little presents. You can buy a set of gorgeous napkins, fold them, iron the design for crispness, wrap them, and give them to your best friend. If you are feeling very creative, embroider a flower, bumblebee, or initials into the corners of the napkins. If you have a sewing machine, stitch a contrasting border around the entire edge. There are a million and one ways you can express yourself with these beautiful little linens. Everyone should have and use them daily. You can sew on beads, attach little round mirrors and brightly colored bits of thread, tie-dye them in your kitchen sink, add a button to one corner and a buttonhole to the opposite corner to create a bib for buttery lobster dinners. Get silly and have a lot of fun; napkins are not expensive.

To make a napkin pocket: fold the top and bottom edges of a square cloth napkin to the center; fold the bottom up again to cover the edges; then fold two sides to the back. If the napkin refuses to keep the shape, simply iron gently as you fold.

Buy a small book on origami (an ancient Asian paper-folding art form), and try to use some of the fun and simple designs on your napkins. There are ways to make boxes to hold bread and croissants.

Sculpted Ice Bowls

Ice bowls can be made ahead of time. They can be any size or shape but the best ones are the simple round ones. They are the most sturdy and last the longest. Don't wait until the night before to start learning how to make them. It does take a couple of tries to get them perfect. Try different fillers and shapes until you find one that you love, then make many of them and always keep them handy. You can store them in the same bowl that you made them in, wrapped in plastic.

Select two glass bowls (or stainless steel). One should fit inside the other with ½ inch to one inch of space between them. Scatter flowers, petals, herbs, or citrus slices in the large bowl. Place the smaller bowl in the larger bowl and tape secure so that the tops of the bowls are flush. Pour water between the bowls to about ½ inch of the top. Add more flowers or other decorations and arrange them with a skewer. Freeze overnight.

Another great way to add to your own design is to add a little food coloring to the water. You can use pink to bring out the color of shrimp, green to bring out the color of an avocado salad, and black to make a grayish bowl for oysters or caviar. Yellow is great for a simple chilled combination of chunks of steamed lobster tossed with lemon mayonnaise on endive leaves.

To release, let the bowls stand at room temperature on a dishtowel for ten to twenty minutes. Do not run under water. Remove the tape, lift out the top bowl, and invert the ice bowl out of the mold. Freeze until ready to use.

A lot of different people have many different favorites. My favorite is a simple round bowl with green food coloring and a good number of mint leaves. This is used for shrimp with lemon slices, scallops in a creamy dill sauce, or stuffed grape leaves from a Greek deli. I like to make a small bowl for each guest, but one larger one is often enough.

Coffee Ice Cubes

Coffee ice cubes are absolutely wonderful for iced coffee. Not only do they look great, but they do not dilute your drink as they melt. I like to keep a tray of these in the back of the freezer (covered with plastic for freshness) just in case. This can also be done with strong tea to use in iced tea on hot summer afternoons.

Pour freshly made coffee (or tea) into ice cube trays. Freeze until solid. Either keep filled trays of ready-to-use cubes in plastic or simply put the cubes into freezer bags to free up the trays.

You can also flavor ice cubes with mint extract, chocolate, cinnamon, rum, orange, etc., depending on the drink that you are serving. Try the mint cubes in summer teas, the cinnamon cubes in iced coffees, and the rum cubes in cola. The chocolate cubes taste wonderful in cola as well. You may also want to put blueberries, raspberries, chunks of pineapple, or pieces of watermelon into your ice cubes with extra flavoring. A giant bowl of punch looks great with pineapple and watermelon ice cubes. A pitcher of margaritas is delicious looking filled with cubes full of little lemon and lime wedges (you could also try yellow and orange gummy worms).

Alternately, deep purple ice cubes look amazing in clear water (they melt, of course, but they look great for the first few minutes. For a tastier effect, try grape juice cubes in clear water, or strawberry juice cubes in lemonade.

You may want to place a whole maraschino cherry inside the cubes. Imagine the fun you could have with them. It takes effort to finally get the cherry out, so you could certainly melt the cubes on each other's skin and the cherry could be the reward. You could also use these cubes in cocktails. Try putting two cherries in each cube.

THE BAR

There is no reason to work through a lengthy bar book only to find that half of what you create tastes horrible. I have selected all the best recipes for you. This is a complete list of the drinks in the seductions for quick reference, as well as many exciting new ones that can be used as alternatives. Also included is a list of some outstanding nonalcoholic drinks that you will find more than make up for the lack of alcohol. These are all guaranteed to please.

For the common household bar you will need:
- Crushed ice
- Metal shaker with strainer top
- 1 oz measure
- Maraschino cherries
- Olives
- Martini glasses (best for most cocktails)
- Large, heavy glass for "rolling" (mix drink in "rolling" cup, then pour it into serving glass with ice and it will mix itself)
- If you can get speed pourer tops for your liquor bottles it will make mixing drinks infinitely easier. A count of four seconds from the speed pourer equals one ounce of liquid.

ALCOHOLIC DRINKS

Almond Soda
In a large glass combine:
Ice
1 oz Crème de Noyeaux (pink almond liqueur)
Soda water

Between the Sheets
In a metal mixing cup combine:
Ice
½ oz brandy
½ oz rum
½ oz triple sec
Shake and strain into martini glass (chill martini glass ahead of time)

Black Orchid Cocktail

In a blender combine:

Crushed ice for two glasses

1 oz vodka

1 oz Blue Curacao

2 oz cranberry juice

Blend

Pour into two tulip glasses

Top with orange juice and lime juice

Black Vodka Teasers

In a pretty decanter combine:

6 oz fine vodka

3 oz sweet and sour mix

3 oz sweetened lime juice

Black food coloring (available in all craft stores and bakery supply shops)

Blow Job

¾ oz Baileys Irish Cream

½ oz butterscotch schnapps

¼ oz Brown Crème de Cocoa

Top with a lot of whip cream

Mix all in a large cup with ice. Stir and strain into a shot glass. Top with whipped cream. Ideally, this drink would be placed on a table and the recipient would have to pick it up with their mouth and drink it all. Some prefer to sip.

Brain Hemorrhage

In a small tumbler ("old-fashioned" glass) combine:

1 ½ oz Baileys Irish Cream

½ oz Grenadine

½ oz 151 Rum

Serve as is

Garnish with whipped cream if desired

Broken Cherry

In a shot glass combine:

½ oz Kahlua

½ oz cream

½ oz cherry brandy

Candy Bar

In a tall glass combine:

Ice

1 oz Kahlua

Fill with orange juice

Champagne Cocktails

In two chilled champagne tulips combine:

1 sugar cube

2 drops bitters

Fill with champagne

Garnish with a twist of lemon peel

Chinese Dream

In a blender combine:

1 oz ginger liqueur

½ oz Kahlua

½ oz White Crème de Cocoa

¼ cup milk

1 scoop vanilla ice cream

Blend these ingredients in a blender until smooth; pour into a large hurricane glass. Add strawberry sauce (an ice cream topping) by pouring down the sides and swirling around edges and sides of glass. Top with whipped cream and shaved chocolate.

Chocolate Chip Cookie Cocktail

In a metal mixing cup combine:

Ice

¾ oz Frangelico

¼ oz White Crème de Cocoa

½ oz cream

Shake and strain into an old-fashioned glass with ice

Chocolate Martini

In a metal mixing cup combine:

Ice

1 oz White Crème de Cocoa

1 oz Brown Crème de Cocoa

2 oz vodka

2 oz cream

Shake and strain into chilled cocktail glass

These are truly the greatest martinis. Decorate cocktail glasses with chocolate ahead of time, and keep in the refrigerator until ready to use. Melt a small amount of chocolate in the microwave in 30 second bursts. Drizzle chocolate in a crisscross pattern inside the glasses, one direction and then the other, perhaps with a different kind of chocolate. Let cool; then put in the refrigerator.

Chocolate Soda

In a tumbler combine:

Ice

1 ½ oz Kahlua

½ oz cream

Fill with coke (pour coke quickly, it will mix the drink)

Concrete Mixer

1 shot of Baileys Irish Cream
1 shot of Rose's lime juice
Mix them in your mouth

Creamsicle Cocktails

In a metal mixing cup combine:
Ice
½ oz vodka
½ oz banana liqueur
1 oz triple sec
1 oz orange juice
3 oz cream

Shake and strain into two chilled cocktail glasses. For extra glimmer, rim the glasses with icing sugar after first dipping in a plate of orange juice.

Fuzzy Navel

In a rolling cup combine:
1 oz peach schnapps
Fill with orange juice
Pour into large tumbler

Golden Cadillac Cocktails

In a metal mixing cup combine:
Ice
1 oz Galliano
1 oz White Crème de Cocoa
4 oz cream
Shake and strain into two chilled cocktail glasses

Grasshopper Cocktails

In a metal mixing cup combine:

Ice

1 oz White Crème de Cocoa

1 oz Green Crème de Menthe

4 oz cream

Shake and strain into two chilled cocktail glasses

Greyhound

In a rolling cup combine:

Ice

1 oz vodka

Fill with grapefruit juice

Pour into large tumbler

(Use salted rim if desired)

Jellybean

In a shot glass combine:

½ oz Anisette or Sambuca

½ oz blackberry brandy

Serve as is

Lavender Rose Martini

In a metal mixing cup combine:

Ice

2 oz good vodka or gin

Splash lavender infusion

Splash rose water

Splash sweetened lime juice

Shake and strain into chilled cocktail glass

Garnish with a small lavender bud and two rose petals

Melon Ball

In a rolling cup combine:

1 oz vodka

Fill with orange juice

Top with ½ oz Midori

Pour into large tumbler

Long Island Iced Tea

In a large glass combine:

Ice

½ oz vodka

½ oz gin

½ oz tequila

½ oz triple sec

½ oz light rum

½ oz sweet and sour mix

Fill with coke

Quickly pour into the serving glass (the drink will mix itself)

Garnish with a lime slice

Mai Tai Cocktails

Chill two large hurricane glasses.

In a mixing cup combine:

Ice

½ oz triple sec

1 oz light rum

½ oz Crème de Almond

½ fill with pineapple juice

½ fill with orange juice

Pour from mixing cup into another large receptacle to mix

Pour into chilled glasses

Top each glass with ½ oz Myers dark rum

Garnish with cherries

Midori Sour Cocktails

Chill two cocktail glasses.

In a metal mixing cup combine:

Ice

2 oz Midori

4 oz sweet and sour mix

Shake and strain in the glasses

Garnish with a mint cherry (or two)

Mimosa

Chill tulip glass and dip the rim of the glass in powdered sugar.

Mix:

½ fresh orange juice

½ chilled champagne

Orange Soda

In a large glass combine:

Ice

1 oz vodka

½ oz triple sec

½ fill with orange juice

½ fill with 7up

Perfect Manhattan

In a metal mixing cup combine:

Ice

1 dash dry vermouth

1 dash sweet vermouth

1¾ oz whiskey

Shake and strain into chilled cocktail glass

Garnish with a lemon twist

Perfect Martini

In a metal mixing cup combine:

Ice

1 dash dry vermouth

1 dash sweet vermouth

1 ¾ oz gin

Shake and strain into chilled cocktail glass and garnish with olives

(Dry Martini has only dry vermouth, and the less vermouth, the drier the martini. A wet martini has only sweet vermouth.)

Pina Colada

In a blender combine:

Crushed ice

1 oz light rum

1 oz coconut cream

2 oz pineapple juice

Blend until smooth. Pour into a hurricane glass. Garnish with a pineapple slice.

Pink Champagne

In a chilled tulip glass combine:

½ oz grenadine

2 drops red food coloring

Fill with chilled champagne

Drop a raspberry or a few currants into it

Pink Squirrel Cocktails

Chill two cocktail glasses.

In a metal mixing cup combine:

Ice

1 oz White Crème de Cocoa

1 oz Crème de Noyeaux

4 oz cream

Shake and strain into the two chilled cocktail glasses

Pink Underpants

In a large glass combine:
Ice
1 oz gin
Fill with pink lemonade
Garnish with a cherry

Planters Punch

In a rolling cup combine:
Ice
1 oz Myers rum
½ oz grenadine
½ oz sweet and sour mix
Fill with orange juice
Dash of Angostura Bitters
Shake and strain into tall glass

Poppers

In a shot glass combine:
1 oz good tequila
Top with 7up

Place hand over top; slam to make it fizz.

Presbyterian

In a rolling cup combine:
Ice
1 oz whiskey
Fill ½ way with tonic
Fill ½ way with ginger ale
Pour into tall glass
Garnish with lemon twist or lime slice

Rum and Cokes

In a large glass combine:

Ice

1 oz rum

Fill with coke

Roll into drinking glass

Screwdriver

In a rolling cup combine:

1 oz vodka

Fill with orange juice

Pour into large tumbler

Sex on the Beach Cocktails

In a large glass combine:

Ice

1 oz vodka

½ oz peach schnapps

½ fill with orange juice

½ fill with cranberry juice

Pour into serving glass

Shock Cocktails

In a metal mixing cup combine:

Ice

1 oz vodka

½ oz triple sec

½ oz lime juice

Shake and strain into two ice-cold shot glasses

If you top this shot with peach schnapps, it will become a tasty treat called a Meltdown. This drink is smoother going down, and it looks prettier, too. Also, this drink can be made to sparkle by adding some edible gold dust to the mixing cup right before pouring.

Stone Sour

In a metal mixing cup combine:
Ice
1 oz apricot brandy
1 oz orange juice
1 oz sweet and sour mix
Shake and strain into chilled cocktail glass

Strawberry Champagne

In a chilled champagne flute combine:
½ strawberry juice or strawberry syrup
½ chilled champagne
Garnish with a sugar coated strawberry

Strawberry Mimosas

In a chilled champagne flute combine:
½ chilled champagne
¼ fresh orange juice
¼ fresh strawberry nectar
Garnish with a strawberry slice and an orange slice

Tequila Sunsets

In a large glass combine:
Ice
1 oz tequila
Fill with orange juice
Top with ½ oz blackberry brandy (add grenadine to make a tequila sunrise)
Pour into serving glass

Tootsie Roll Cocktails

In a large, heavy glass combine:
Ice
1 oz Kahlua
Fill with orange juice
Pour into serving glass

Watermelon Shot

In a shot glass combine:
½ oz Southern Comfort
½ oz Crème de Noyeaux
½ oz watermelon schnapps
Top with 7up
Serve as is

Watermelon Champagne

In a chilled champagne flute combine:
1 oz watermelon schnapps
½ oz Crème de Noyeaux
Fill with chilled champagne

Garnish with a sugar-coated strawberry, and rim the glass with lemon juice.

White Chocolate Raspberry Liqueur

1 oz Godiva White Chocolate Liqueur
1 oz Chambord
½ oz Maraschino liqueur
1 oz cream

Mix the Godiva and the cream together in a small pitcher. Mix the Chambord and the Maraschino in another. Chill them both until ready to serve. Pour into chilled cordial glasses at exactly the same time. This is the creamiest, dreamiest dessert liqueur that you have ever tasted. I can assure you that you will want to have this wonderful potion in your refrigerator at all times.

COFFEE AND TEA DRINKS

For all coffee drinks, use only very hot and very fresh coffee. If you use a glass coffee mug, bear in mind that you must first put a metal spoon in the mug or the glass may break when you pour the coffee. Use freshly whipped cream if you can, and top with a sprinkle of raw sugar or powdered sugar.

Chocolate Coffee

In a coffee mug combine:

1 oz chocolate liqueur or Crème de Cocoa

½ oz Kahlua

Fill with hot coffee

Heartwarming Tea

2 cups spearmint leaves, dry and finely chopped

¾ cup dried lemon peel

2 tbsp candied gingerroot, finely diced

½ cup cloves

1 tbsp anise seeds

Mix all the ingredients well, and place in a large tea jar. Keep by your stove; the warmth will only enhance the flavors. To make: use one teaspoon per person plus an extra teaspoon for the pot, and let it steep in boiling water for five minutes. Strain into teacups. Serve with raw sugar cubes and a twist of lemon rind. This recipe is absolutely pleasing; make some for yourself and keep it handy, as you will drink it often.

Irish Coffee

In a coffee mug combine:

1 sugar cube

½ oz Baileys Irish Cream

½ oz Irish whiskey

Fill with hot coffee

Add cream if necessary

Mexican Coffee

In a coffee mug combine:

½ oz tequila

½ oz Kahlua

Fill with hot coffee

Rose Petal Tea

Wash several rose petals and crush them with the back of a spoon. Mix the petals with a favorite loose tea (peppermint and lemon teas are the most compatible with the subtle rose flavor).

Spanish Coffee

In a coffee mug combine:

½ oz brandy

½ oz Kahlua

Fill with hot coffee

Traditional Dutch Coffee

In a coffee mug combine:

1 sugar cube, white or brown sugar

1 oz chocolate syrup

hot fresh coffee

1 broken cardamon seed (These are available at any supermarket in the spice aisle. They are large seeds that pack a lot of punch. The flavor is intense. To use them in coffee and in other foods, bite into a seed to release the flavor and let it soak in the coffee or sauce for a few minutes)

Let sit for a few minutes, stir, then serve.

NONALCOHOLIC COCKTAILS

Aspic Cocktail

Use clear, unflavored gelatin mix to make an aspic out of tomato juice.

In a martini glass:

Half-fill glass with cubes of the tomato gelatin

Fill with tomato and vegetable juice

Garnish with an olive

Balsamic Vinegar Tincture

In a chilled, tall glass combine:

Ice

Two or three drops fine quality balsamic or champagne vinegar

Fill with seltzer water

Garnish with lime slices

Cherry Cokes

Add one ounce cherry-flavored syrup to a glass of icy cola and stir only once to mix. Top with an extra cherry. Use almost any other flavor to create another taste.

Easy Breezy Smoothies

In a blender combine:

1 cup frozen chunks of any fruit (melons like honeydew and cantaloupe are great)

½ cup vanilla frozen yogurt

1 tbsp honey

blend to smooth

Garnish with large straws

You may mix any combination of fruits and try other flavors of frozen yogurt.

ACCOMPANIMENT FOR SMOOTHIES

Tiny ice cream sandwiches: Take apart cookies such as Oreos, Nutter Butters, and vanilla crème cookies. Place a tiny scoop of ice cream that has been thawing at room temperature for fifteen minutes. Put cookies back together. These can be done with any flavor of ice cream or sorbet.

Forbidden Virgin Punch

In a tumbler combine:

1 oz guava nectar

1 oz orange juice

1 tsp honey

Fill with cream soda

Garnish with a red licorice vine (this can also be used as a straw).

Fresh Flower Water

To glasses of ice water, add a bunch of washed and trimmed pansies. The pansy is the most commonly used and the prettiest of all the edible flowers, but you can easily find others.

Grapefruit Frappe

In a blender combine:

1 cup ice

1 cup fresh grapefruit juice

2 tbsp confectioner's sugar

1 tbsp grenadine

Blend until pureed and smooth. Transfer to a thermos.

Green Fantasia Cocktail

In a large, chilled glass combine:

Ice

1 oz orange juice

1 oz grenadine

Fill most of the way with pineapple juice

Top with a splash of green syrup (shaved ice syrups work nicely for these colorful cocktails)

Honey Water

In a large, chilled glass combine:

Ice

1 tsp honey

2 drops rose infusion

1 drop orange water

Fill with ice water

The rose infusion and orange water are available at most fine liquor stores. They are nonalcoholic but many use them to delicately flavor water and tea.

Ker Supreme

In a metal mixing cup combine:

Ice

6 oz nonalcoholic white zinfandel

Dash of raspberry syrup

Dash of lemon juice

Garnish with raspberries

Lavender Tea Infusion

In a large glass combine:

2 oz strong tea

A few drops lavender infusion

1 tsp honey

Fill with sparkling water

Garnish with a lavender bud or mint leaf

Lively Lime Nonalcoholic Wine Seltzer

Run the rim of a wine glass in some corn syrup or honey with lime juice.

In a glass combine:

2 oz nonalcoholic white wine

Fill with lime soda

Garnish with three thin slices of lime

Molasses Shake

In a blender combine:

1 tsp molasses

8 oz cold milk

A small handful of ice

Blend until pureed, and top the milkshake with whipped cream and caramel sauce. Serve with cheesecake.

Orange Spree

In a metal mixing cup combine:

Ice

3 oz nonalcoholic white zinfandel

3 oz orange juice

Shake and strain into a wine glass

Top with a dash of angostura bitters and an twist of orange peel

Pink Cherry Lemonade

In a large glass combine:

Ice

1 oz cherry syrup (for shaved ice or Italian sodas)

Fill with pink lemonade

Garnish with maraschino cherries

Pomegranate Juice

You can buy unfiltered pomegranate juice at Persian markets. Serve chilled in a wine glass.

Rosewine Spritzer

In a large glass combine:

Ice

¼ cup nonalcoholic red wine

Fill with soda water

Add a handful of rose petals and chill for thirty minutes before serving

Samba Juice

In a metal mixing cup combine:

Ice

1 oz guava juice

1 oz pineapple juice

1 oz apple juice

1 tbsp lime juice

1 tbsp cream of coconut

Shake and strain into chilled cocktail glass

Garnish with a slice of pineapple

Shirley Temple

A great alternative if you do not want alcohol. Add a dash of grenadine to a glass of lemon-lime soda. Garnish with two thin red straws and maraschino cherries.

Sunset Sweets

In two small glasses combine:

Ice

Fill mostly full with orange juice or orange soda

Top with 1 oz grenadine

Garnish with three cherries

Sweet Peach Seltzer

Fill two chilled champagne tulips with one-half chilled peach nectar sweetened with a teaspoon of honey, and one-half seltzer water. Garnish with a slice of fresh peach. Before filling, rub the rims of the glasses with a lemon wedge and then run through a little powdered sugar.

Tropical Bliss

In a metal mixing cup combine:

Ice

1 oz lemon lime soda

2 oz pineapple juice

1 oz maraschino cherry juice

1 oz apricot nectar

1 tsp lime juice

Shake and strain into chilled cocktail glass

Garnish with a banana slice on the rim

Virgin Amaretto Sours

Chill two cocktail glasses

In a metal mixing cup combine:

Ice

½ oz almond syrup

3 oz orange juice

Dash of grenadine for color

Shake and strain into glass. Garnish with an orange twist or candied orange peel (available at any fine chocolate boutique).

Virgin Bliss

In a tall, chilled glass combine:

Ice

1 oz coconut milk

1 oz cream

4 oz or so apricot nectar

Stir and garnish with a halved apricot

Virgin Ginger Tart

In a large glass combine:

Ice

Fill with ½ sweet and sour mix and ½ ginger ale

Transfer to chilled serving glass

Virgin Passion Cocktail

In a metal mixing cup combine:

1 oz sweet and sour mix

1 oz grenadine

3 oz passion fruit nectar

Shake and strain into a chilled cocktail glass. Garnish with a mint leaf.

Virgin Peach Fuzzy

In a chilled wine glass combine:

1 slice of fresh peach

2 oz peach nectar

Fill with ice cold ginger ale

White Grape Spritzer

In a glass carafe combine:

½ white grape juice

½ seltzer water

A handful of washed, halved white grapes

Serve the carafe at tableside, and drink out of wine glasses.

QUICK REFERENCE
ASTROLOGY

This is obviously not the best way to decide upon a mate, and it is, by no means, the most accurate source of information. But it is fun, and you may notice some strong similarities between this reference and how things progress between the two of you. Have fun and be open-minded.

First, you will be provided a brief summary for each sign, followed by a compatibility passage for each prospective mate. You can use this information when deciding upon a gift, when making travel plans, or simply when choosing what flowers to adorn the kitchen table with.

 AQUARIUS: (January 20–February 19)
Independent, sincere, generous, eccentric, friendly, detached
Lacks: accuracy, efficiency, tact
Colors: blues, mixtures of blues
Stones: opal, sapphire
Flowers: fruit blossoms, pansies
Foods: olives, mangos, figs, melons
Trouble Body Parts: the legs, the feet
Should Visit: Arabia, Sweden

PISCES: (February 19–March 21)
Poetic, imaginative, understanding, emotional, gentle, adaptable, intuitive, loyal, tolerant
Lacks: decisiveness, determination, logic, stability
Colors: blue-green, violet, sparkling, iridescent white
Stones: aquamarine, jade, tourmaline, amethyst
Flowers: orchid, water lily
Foods: raisins, pears, apricots
Trouble Body Parts: the feet, the back
Should Visit: Europe, Scandinavia

ARIES: (March 21–April 20)

Assertive, active, impulsive, energetic, forceful, alert

Lacks: control, moderation, tolerance, humility, patience, restraint

Color: bright red

Stones: diamond, ruby

Flowers: poppy, geranium

Foods: dates, sunflower seeds, onions

Trouble Body Part: the head

Should Visit: England, Israel

TAURUS: (April 20–May 21)

Persistent, conservative, patient, possessive, stable

Lacks: adaptability, imagination, forgiveness

Colors: orange, pink, Easter pastels

Stones: agate, emerald

Flowers: daisy, daffodil, lily

Foods: spinach, radish, carrot

Trouble Body Parts: the neck, the shoulders

Should Visit: Ireland, Australia

GEMINI: (May 21–June 21)

Inquisitive, alert, witty, restless, intellectual, original

Lacks: patience, concentration, sympathy

Colors: orange, violet, pale blue, yellow

Stones: beryl, crystal

Flowers: lavender, wild flowers, dried flowers

Foods: melons, blueberries, pineapple

Trouble Body Parts: the hands, the lungs

Should Visit: Belgium and Egypt

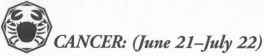 **CANCER: (June 21–July 22)**

Sensitive, romantic, dependable, protective, cautious, timid, moody

Lacks: assertiveness, logic, daring

Colors: green, orange-red, all iridescent hues

Stones: moonstone, opal, pearl

Flowers: honeysuckle, water lily

Foods: kale, watercress, herbs

Trouble Body Parts: the digestive organs, the breasts

Should Visit: Africa, Scotland

 **LEO: (July 22–Aug 23)**

Creative, dramatic, proud, broad-minded, dignified, loyal, generous, optimistic

Lacks: humility, versatility, sensitivity, thrift

Colors: yellow, orange, gold

Stones: diamond, ruby, cat's-eye

Flowers: sunflower, orange blossoms, marigold, poppy

Foods: nuts, bananas, papaya

Trouble Body Parts: the heart, spine

Should Visit: France, Italy, Sicily

 VIRGO: (August 23–September 23)

Analytical, practical, skeptical, methodical, meticulous, calculating, orderly

Lacks: tolerance, optimism, confidence, openmindedness

Colors: yellow-green, deep blue

Stones: jasper, agate

Flowers: narcissus, lily of the valley

Foods: cranberry, avocado, currants

Trouble Body Part: the intestines

Should Visit: Switzerland, Austria

LIBRA: (September 23–October 23)

Rational, friendly, considerate, artistic, helpful, idealistic, tolerant

Lacks: firmness, independence, depth, directness

Colors: green, chartreuse, blue

Stones: carnelian, coral

Flowers: lily, pansy

Foods: coconut, meat, whole grains

Trouble Body Parts: the kidneys

Should Visit: China, Tibet

 SCORPIO: (October 23–November 22)

Intense, sensual, passionate, enigmatic, mysterious, energetic

Lacks: forgiveness, openness, cooperation

Colors: luminous colors, maroon

Stones: bloodstone, topaz

Flowers: thistle, heather

Foods: cauliflower, guava, kale

Trouble Body Parts: the sex organs, the colon

Should Visit: Morocco, Iceland

 SAGITTARIUS: (November 22–December 21)

Optimistic, restless, inquisitive, spontaneous, friendly, athletic

Lacks: restraint, sincerity, tact, realism, responsibility

Colors: rich, deep hues such as deep purple and deep red

Stones: turquoise, garnet

Foods: shrimp, artichoke, herbs

Trouble Body Parts: the hips, the thighs

Should Visit: Hungary, Argentina

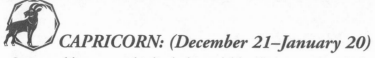

CAPRICORN: *(December 21–January 20)*

Serious, diligent, methodical, dependable, determined, orderly

Lacks: sociability, optimism, generosity, playfulness

Colors: indigo, blue-black, sage green

Stones: garnet, jet

Flowers: sunflower, black poppy

Foods: nuts, milk, cheese

Trouble Body Parts: the knees, the hair

Should Visit: Mexico, Greece

COMPATIBILITY GUIDE

Aquarius

Aquarius–Aquarius. This combination will have many surprises for both. Each will understand the other's need for a certain amount of freedom and will gladly give it. There will always be plenty to talk about, since both are interested in how things would be in an ideal world.

Aquarius–Pisces. This arrangement will help sensitize the Aquarius sexually and romantically, and help the Pisces become less acutely sensitive. Pisces should understand that unpredictability is an Aquarian characteristic, and the Aquarian should give the Pisces room to dream.

Aquarius–Aries. Both of these signs search out great adventures, and there will never be a lack of conversation. The only hurdle that may pop up is the need for more cooperation in everyday life.

Aquarius–Taurus. Taurean jealousy could seriously impair this couple's chances as Aquarians have a great need for freedom. On top of this, both signs have a tendency to be stubborn. If the Taurus can melt the iceberg façade of the Aquarius, and the Aquarius can teach the Taurus some much-needed detachment, the two will have a wonderful time together for a very long time.

Aquarius–Gemini. These two will come together on all levels, including friendship, interests, and romance. The underlying friendship will be even more important to these two than the sex, which will sizzle. These two should always be careful not to let their intellectual activities stifle their emotional needs. If they can balance these areas of life out, they will have a terrific time together.

Aquarius–Cancer. The Aquarius may need a little coaxing to come to bed, but once there these two will be very sexually compatible. In everyday life, the Aquarius needs to realize that the

Cancer needs some privacy, and if their basic beliefs are the same, this will be a great and long-lasting relationship.

Aquarius–Leo. If this relationship leads to marriage, it will be a very successful one. Both signs are very loyal. They are, unfortunately, also stubborn, and they will have to work to avoid friction. The Leo will want to run things, and the Aquarius will want personal freedom of action and a less possessive atmosphere.

Aquarius–Virgo. Genuine friendship can grow into love. After they become lovers, or even marry, friendship will still be the predominating factor in the relationship. Both signs are very mentally oriented and are independent, and the Aquarius needs to take care not to neglect the needs of the Virgo. The Virgo will need for them to spend at least a couple of nights a week alone together.

Aquarius–Libra. These signs will find much to talk about, although the Libra may seem conservative compared to the far-out notions of the Aquarius. They will establish a great sexual connection, and there is excellent potential for a good marriage. These two signs have a great deal in common and will do everything together.

Aquarius–Scorpio. This will be a very intense relationship. Sexually, though, the Aquarius is more casual and open than the Scorpio. Both will have to learn to be a little more considerate of the others needs. The Aquarius will resist any possessiveness on the part of the Scorpio, and this will help the Scorpio deal with temptation realistically.

Aquarius–Sagittarius. This pair will have much in common. Both have a sense of detachment, and there is a sense of agreement that a clingy relationship is unacceptable. These two will greatly enjoy each other's interest in broader social and philosophical issues.

Aquarius–Capricorn. This relationship works because the Capricorn can use being shaken up a bit, which is what the Aquarius does best with their flashy and demonstrative temperament. The ongoing relationship will have to make allowances for the fact that the Capricorn likes a good deal of order, and the Aquarius never likes to be pinned down to anything that even resembles a schedule.

Pisces

Pisces–Pisces. This pair will understand each other deeper than the need to talk about it, and will be acutely sensitive to each other's moods, even when not together. Two Pisceans in a good mood can shoot each other ecstatically out of this world, and likewise two depressed Pisceans can put each other into a very deep slump. They must try to protect each other from their own emotions. If they can, they can share a lifetime of beautiful dreams.

Pisces–Aries. The Aries may move too quickly for the shy Pisces at first, and the Pisces may wait too long to show interest. The Aries needs to realize that Pisces need to be allowed to feel relaxed in order to feel romantic. Pressure in the relationship for more excitement may become a problem. The Pisces would like to languish in bed all day together, and the Aries would rather be skiing. This can be a wonderful pairing if the Aries calms down and the Pisces is outdoorsy.

Pisces–Taurus. On a practical level, these two will not have an easy time of it. The Pisces is constantly changing directions, and this can drive the Taurus nuts. A Pisces can appreciate such a down-to-earth partner, however, and if married, they will be devoted mates.

Pisces–Gemini. Both of these signs long to be "truly in love," and they both have split personalities as signs. This pairing will be a bit confusing to both. Luckily, they are both easygoing and patient; this may save the relationship time and time again. The Pisces must realize that the Gemini's tendency to talk about everything that happens is their way of expressing affection, and not an attempt to grab all the attention.

Pisces–Cancer. This can be an ideal romantic relationship. Sexually there will be a very strong attraction that will reinforce the couple's emotional compatibility. They may find it a bit hard to be practical, as both tend to live in fantasy. If they learn to thoroughly talk things out they will be able to deal with little annoyances of humdrum daily life and then get back to dreaming.

Pisces–Leo. This can be a confusing relationship for the Leo. Sometimes the Pisces will wholeheartedly respond to the Leo's generous warmth, and sometimes will seem to cut off the Leo completely. The Leo might sooner or later lose patience and that could be the end of the affair. The Pisces tends to nurture and sympathize, and the Leo always loves the attention. Also, most Pisceans need protection, which is something that the Leo loves to give. If the Leo can be a little more patient, this will be a sweet and loving arrangement.

Pisces–Virgo. This is a good pairing. If there is any sign that can flow with Virgo moods, it is Pisces. The Virgo, above all, needs the warmth and understanding that the Pisces can give, and Virgo finds it easy to relax and dream with a Pisces lover. The Virgo loves the opportunity to work out the details of the Pisces' life. They also help each other in those areas where one is stronger than the other is—the Pisces in creativity and the Virgo in practical ability.

Pisces–Libra. This pair will be sensitive to each others' needs and can enhance each others' natural awareness of beauty. They will have to learn to discuss problems out in the open, as both signs tend to hold it in. Also, both signs have a procrastinating nature and must fight together to overcome that, especially if married. All in all, it is a great combination.

Pisces–Scorpio. Both signs have the potential for a deep emotional understanding of each other. There will be a strong intuitive connection between the two. The understanding nature of the Pisces can keep the Scorpio from being overly suspicious, and the Scorpio can protect the Pisces from being imposed upon. The Pisces will need to express what he is feeling, and the Scorpio must not give in to playing emotional games with the Pisces.

Pisces–Sagittarius. Both are dreamers, and the romance between them will take on a dream-like quality. The Sagittarius must understand that the Pisces holds things inside, and the Pisces must understand that the Sagittarius' natural bluntness does not stem from malice.

Pisces–Capricorn. The Capricorn serves as a much-needed anchor for the ethereal and impractical Pisces. The Pisces needs to understand that, romantically and sexually, the affections of the Capricorn burn more like a steady flame rather than a fireworks display. The Capricorn should realize that simply expressing feelings will mean a great deal to the Pisces. Both signs very much enjoy being quiet together.

Aries

Aries–Aries. These two will fall in love at first sight. Although, sometimes sex will be the main preoccupation for an Aries. The problem with many Aries affairs is that they are quick to begin and even quicker to end. This will be a relationship full of fun and excitement, but short in temper. With a little less selfishness on both sides, this can become a stable and lasting relationship.

Aries–Taurus. These two have different outlooks on love and marriage. Aries are liberated in terms of sex, and Taureans are much more conservative. To an Aries, marriage will not seem natural, and once married, the Aries may always have a roving eye.

Aries–Gemini. Aries has met his match. Both signs are bent toward sexual freedom. Gemini, however, will add and cultivate a deep level of friendship within the love relationship. If they do get married, it will definitely be a richly rewarding and very exciting marriage with never a dull moment. These two will never get into a rut, and will always have plenty to talk about.

Aries–Cancer. This relationship will need a lot of mutual tolerance. The Cancer can be moody and unpredictable, and the Aries will not like it. The Cancer, however, can give the Aries the nurturing that they can't create for themselves. The Aries bursts of temper can be very painful to the Cancer.

Aries–Leo. There must be understanding on both sides for this to work. Because of the raging temper of the Aries, there will be many scenes in both private and public. Although, these quarrels are usually quickly resolved and lead to a deeper mutual understanding. This can be a healthy relationship.

Aries–Virgo. The Aries will fall in love at first sight while the Virgo will think awhile before diving in headfirst. If the Aries can keep his hands off long enough to stimulate intellectually as well, then this can be a wonderful relationship. First and foremost, they must establish a balance between the spontaneity of the Aries and the Virgo tendency to put off decisions until there is no way to avoid them.

Aries–Libra. The Aries will bring passion and enthusiasm to the relationship, and the Libra will add kindness and sympathy. Both signs are romantics, so this is a perfect pairing. The Aries needs to understand that a deep and permanent relationship is ultimately what the Libra has in mind, and that may not be what the independent Aries wants right now.

Aries–Scorpio. This relationship will be very intense, possibly too intense. The Aries will meet their match with the fiery Scorpio. This may have all the earmarks of an on-off relationship, and it will be difficult to maintain. These two will soon find that they can't live with each other, and they can't live without each other. This could be a great match if they can show more commitment.

Aries–Sagittarius. This will be a very energetic couple. They will find many outdoor adventures. This will be a close and warm relationship with no secrets or resentment on either side. A perfect pairing, indeed.

Aries–Capricorn. The calm, stable nature of the Capricorn blends well with the Aries' zest for life. An Aries needs a steadying point, which the Capricorn provides. In order for this relationship to be a lasting one, however, the Aries needs to understand the Capricorn's need for a certain amount of routine, and the Capricorn must make allowances for the erratic qualities of the Aries.

Taurus

Taurus–Taurus. Two Tauruses may find their soul mates in each other. They will share a sensuous and considerate approach to lovemaking, and they will bond very deeply. These two will naturally be drawn to marriage. They will feel perhaps a little too comfortable with each other, like an old couple. They must learn to not be stubborn and to try new things to keep the relationship alive.

Taurus–Gemini. To a Gemini, sex means creating a deeper friendship, and the Taurus may feel that this means they are detached, emotionally. The Taurus may be bewildered when the Gemini asks, "Can we just be friends?" In a lasting relationship, the Taurus can give the Gemini the stability they need, and the Gemini can keep the Taurus from settling into ruts.

Taurus–Cancer. The erratic Cancer can be passionate one moment and turned off the next. This will be aided by the Taurus's ability to make them feel more secure emotionally. This can be a great relationship as both partners desire to nurture each other and to have a secure home.

Taurus–Leo. Leos can be very conventional and proper, which creates some problems. A Taurus can capture a reluctant Leo by catering to his ego, and the Taurus will find the Leo very attentive and loyal. This pair makes a great marriage, and is very loving and supportive.

Taurus–Virgo. A Virgo's approach to love is more on the intellectual side, and the Taurus has his share of commonsense, so this is a great pairing. The easygoing Taurus can calm the jittery nature of the Virgo, and the two will share in all domestic responsibilities, as they are both fastidious.

Taurus–Libra. Libras are often "in love with love." The Taurus will respond wholeheartedly, and the Libra may not know what to do next. This relationship can fulfill the need for a settled tie that both Venus-related signs have.

Taurus–Scorpio. This is a bit like walking an emotional tightrope. They can be exciting and passionate, but also extremely stubborn. Scorpio jealousy and Taurean possessiveness might create a tense situation to say the least. This will work only if both learn to relax with each other and make a conscious effort of it. The Scorpio may take the Taurus to new heights of passion. They will be complementary to each other or be complete opposites.

Taurus–Sagittarius. In order for this to work, a lot of patience will be required. Taureans can be very possessive, and the Sagittarius needs freedom. This will work if a sense of change and adventure prevails from time to time.

Taurus–Capricorn. These two will be practical, realistic, and enduring. The Capricorn will be able to keep the Taurus from getting stuck in laziness. This will be a good marriage, and it will be even better if the two are in a business relationship where they will work side by side.

Gemini

Gemini–Gemini. These two will be very in tune sexually. Only another Gemini can fathom the deep complex interrelationship of romance and intellectual stimulation that a Gemini needs. No matter where the romance progresses, there will always be an underlying element of genuine friendship between them.

Gemini–Cancer. As lovers, these two have a fifty-fifty chance. Sexually, completely different things stimulate them. The Gemini is stimulated intellectually, and the Cancer is engulfed by a sudden passion. Although they both very much enjoy sex, they may not feel like it at the same time.

Gemini–Leo. This pair may just succeed because the relationship offers a challenge to both. The Gemini can get beneath the layer of pomposity and discover the passion of the Leo. The warmth of the Leo may break down the tough mental barriers that the Gemini puts up. This may very well lead to marriage, but the Gemini must learn not to hurry the slower-paced Leo.

Gemini–Virgo. This relationship may be in danger of too much communication. The Gemini's frequent changes of direction, and the Virgo's tendency to criticize will be irritants. If they can overcome the tendency to project onto each other their own changeability, they will find that they have much in common.

Gemini–Libra. These two are always off to a good start, and they will find the perfect balance of mental and emotional traits in a lover. The Gemini knows that the romantic Libra will appreciate an occasional sentimental gift. Both signs will feel a deep, trusting friendship between them. This should work out very well for both.

Gemini–Scorpio. These two operate on two completely different emotional levels. The intense Scorpio can irritate the less intense, more casually romantic Gemini. The poor Scorpio will feel that the Gemini is cool and unemotional. This assumption is incorrect, but it may drive a wedge between them.

Gemini–Sagittarius. These two will have an immediate and strong attraction for each other. Both signs tend to treasure a strong bond of friendship in a relationship. The Sagittarius will lend wisdom to the Gemini, and the Gemini will provide the Sagittarius with the information they need to build their overview of life.

Gemini–Capricorn. These two will be very passionate, but there will be difficulties. Although the Gemini can be carefree with their attentions, the Capricorn may feel that this aloofness means too much space between them. The Gemini's spirited approach to life may inspire the Capricorn to lighten up and keep from getting stuck in a routine.

Cancer

Cancer–Cancer. These two are highly sensitive, and this can create an atmosphere of negativity. They will have an instinctual appreciation for each other's good qualities, particularly the constant affection they both thrive on. They may become almost telepathic in the way that they are always on the same wavelength. Both partners should strive to lighten the climate of the relationship, though.

Cancer–Leo. This is one of the warmest combinations in the zodiac. The Leo male tends to almost be a kindly father figure to his sweetheart, although any Leo may be a bit domineering for the sensitivities of the Cancer. These two must stay aware of their individual sexual needs, as the Leo is very direct and basic, and the Cancer needs a more delicate approach. Keep this in mind, and this will be a very enduring and very sensual relationship.

Cancer–Virgo. These two mesh very well romantically. The Virgo will allow the affair to develop at just the right pace as the Cancer is easily panicked. There will be a sharing of household responsibilities, and a marriage between these two will be very satisfying for both.

Cancer–Libra. The Libra will quickly learn what the Cancer needs to be fulfilled emotionally, as Libras are chameleons and always take on some characteristics of their partners. These two share an enthusiasm for life and love, and will most likely form a solid long-term relationship.

Cancer–Scorpio. Both signs are very sensitive, and this can lead to one or both partners becoming withdrawn emotionally. There will be inevitable rough spots. However, the passionate energy of the Scorpio can broaden the Cancer's approach to sex and let them loosen up, and the Cancer can teach the Scorpio sympathy and generosity of feeling. If these hurdles can be overcome, this will be an excellent marriage combination.

Cancer–Sagittarius. This relationship takes a lot of compromising. These two will be very compatible in bed, but will annoy each other in everyday life. The Sagittarius will want to lead an active social life, and the Cancer will usually want to stay home and relax. The Sagittarius may be able to bring the Cancer out of "down" moods, and the Cancer can help the Sagittarius be more aware of his feelings.

Cancer–Capricorn. This will be a stimulating, long-lasting relationship. Even though disagreements will usually be resolved in bed, which is fine for these two, both need to understand that there is an underlying serious matter, and it will be better for the relationship if they take the time to talk about it. Both need to take life a little less seriously and realize that this is really the only reason that they ever fight.

Leo

Leo–Leo. Leos have a strong sex drive, so most of this couple's time will be taken up by lovemaking. These two must be able to share the spotlight so as not to damage the other's ego, though. If they can do this, there will be great tranquility, and they will spread good cheer to everyone around them.

Leo–Virgo. There aren't many characters that are as completely different as these two signs. Leo is very warm, in love and in bed, while the Virgo is very detached, finding it difficult to express his emotions. This coupling may be good for the Virgo, though, as the Leo may be able to make their chilly partner realize that they do have a romantic side. The Leo may benefit from the Virgo's natural penchant for service that will mesh nicely with Leo's regal side. These two should try to periodically reverse these roles, though.

Leo–Libra. These two are different in many ways, but are very sexually suited. In the long-term, the notorious Leo temper will be the biggest hurdle. The Leo may not understand why the Libra is still upset after the outburst. The Leo may be put off by the Libra's inability to make up his mind.

Leo–Scorpio. This relationship promises plenty of sex, but will most likely have problems in other areas. The Leo's extravagance will irritate the Scorpio's overcritical nature. Also, Scorpios tend to be jealous, which will deeply bother the Leo, who tends to be friendly and flirtatious.

Leo–Sagittarius. Both signs are good-natured, loving, and enthusiastic about sex. It can be a good, solid relationship. Leos need to remember that the Sagittarius needs a good deal of freedom. The Leo can take comfort in knowing that the Sagittarius will never be jealous.

Leo–Capricorn. Here is another combination of rather different people. Leos have a profound sense of humor when it comes to sex, so they will joke and tease a lot about it; this will not sit well with the more serious Capricorn. Leos are completely devoted to the care of their partner, so there is no sign better suited to warming up the Capricorn. The Capricorn can help the Leo become aware of when he is overemphasizing the playful side of life.

Virgo

Virgo–Virgo. When Virgo meets Virgo, there will not be a "head-over-heels" infatuation. The affair will have to develop slowly and cautiously. By the time they are "in love," they will have both fully analyzed each other's virtues and failings and weighed the pros and cons of the relationship. Despite this, they can be very enthusiastic in bed. These two seem just about perfect together.

Virgo–Libra. Neither will ever run out of conversation, although the Libra tends to be a bit more romantic than the Virgo. With persistence, the Libra will be able to get the Virgo to relax and enjoy having sex as well as enjoy being in love. The Virgo can help the Libra counteract his occasional lazy streak.

Virgo–Scorpio. These two are at opposite ends of the emotional spectrum. The Virgo is cool and detached, while the Scorpio is very passionate and intense. This means that the two must show a great deal of understanding and patience. These two must learn from each other to grow. The thorniest problem might be the basic difference in sexual needs. This can be resolved as both share thoroughness and the need to get to the bottom of any problem.

Virgo–Sagittarius. This will be the best thing that ever happened to the Virgo. The Sagittarius will inspire the Virgo. The Sagittarian's love of life will infect the Virgo with enthusiasm. To the Virgo, though, the Sagittarius will seem messy and disorganized, and his emotional level will be somewhat different. If they can meet in the middle, they will be a fantastic combination.

Virgo–Capricorn. This will be a low-key but harmonious relationship. Each will have to deal with moodiness and occasional depression, but both signs tend to come around to common sense before long. They will enjoy projects together. This pair makes a good long-term relationship.

Libra

Libra–Libra. These two have a beautiful natural communication. Each will make a special effort to please the other. They are also likely to develop a great sexual communication. In a long-term relationship, they will have to learn not to blame each other for the decisions they make together. They should also try to bring disagreements to the surface without being competitive.

Libra–Scorpio. These two will either completely repel each other, or be two equal and complementary halves. There is nothing in between. The naturally decisive Scorpio can help the Libra to be more so. The Libra can help the sharp-tongued Scorpio add grace to his speech.

Libra–Sagittarius. These two will enjoy social activities together, as well as working together. They are very well matched, although the Libra may try to cling a little more than the Sagittarius likes. In an ongoing relationship, their home will become a gathering place for friends, and a place of charm where many feel welcome.

Libra–Capricorn. These two are likely to be extremely talkative, although the Capricorn will be the better listener. Sexually, the affectionate Libra can balance the cool but intense Capricorn. The Capricorn will help the Libra organize, and the Libra can help the Capricorn balance out his tendency toward too much overdrive.

Scorpio

Scorpio–Scorpio. Emotionally and sexually, this will be an intense combination. Probably this is the most intense combination in the zodiac. They must guard against the temptation to continually test each other's intentions. Once they trust each other, however, their relationship will be a deeply meaningful one.

Scorpio–Sagittarius. These two are much better off as lovers than merely friends. The Scorpio looks into the emotional depths of a situation while the Sagittarius accepts things at their face value. In a permanent relationship between these two, the Scorpio should understand that being with a Sagittarius can open up some closed doors to the psyche that may need airing out. The

Sagittarius will find that being with a Scorpio will increase his emotional awareness.

Scorpio–Capricorn. This is a good combination in many ways. Emotionally and sexually, the Scorpio should be able to probe underneath the Capricorn's exterior to the strong and earthy desires. The Capricorn has more driving intensity to achieve his goals, and the Scorpio has more emotional strength, so these two balance each other out nicely. They share a great sense of humor as well.

Sagittarius

Sagittarius–Sagittarius. This is a super adventurous pair, ready to explore sex and romance with plenty of good humor. They will enjoy sports, and will work well together. There should be an element of independence and romance kept on a light tone. Sagittarius do not get into heavy love drama, but they will definitely have many long, deep conversations on what the world is all about.

Sagittarius-Capricorn: This will be wonderful if they can understand their differences. The Sagittarius can bring out the smoldering fire under the layers of the Capricorn both emotionally and sexually. The Capricorn can serve as a much-needed anchor point for the Sagittarius, who is much more likely to let his enthusiasm take over. The Capricorn should take care not to throw too much cold water on the Sagittarius' dream.

Capricorn

Capricorn-Capricorn: There will be love here, even if neither is overly demonstrative. Both Capricorns have a basic need for solitude, and combining this with togetherness can be tricky. They will find it easy to pursue different interests in the same room, yet tune into each other periodically. Neither will be temperamental, or sloppy, or tend to lose things—three things a Capricorn cannot stand.

AROMASEXUALITY

This additional information will most certainly come in handy in choosing the perfect essential oil for any occasion.

Essential Oil	Healing Effects on the Soul	Healing Effects on the Body	Fragrance
Grapefruit	Relieves Depression and Anxiety	Astringent	Citrus
Lemongrass	Relaxing, Sleep Inducing	Relieves Minor Aches, Pains, and Headaches	Herbal Lemon
Eucalyptus	Energizing, Uplifting	Good for Respiratory System	Fresh, Sharp, Medicinal
Ginger	Eases Confusion, Comforting, Erotic	Good For Motion Sickness and Anxiety	Spicy, Dominant
Basil	Uplifting, Energizing	Relieves Muscle Spasms	Warm, Spicy, Herbal
Lavender	Soothing, Refreshing, Brings Balance	Rejuvenates Skin Tone, Relieves Headaches	Clean, Arousing, Strong
Nutmeg	Uplifting for the Mind, Imparts Creativity	Relieves Minor Joint Pain	Arousing, Sharp Spice
Orange	Heightens Senses, Soothes Uneasy Spirits	Disinfectant, Good for Skin	Citrus
Tea Tree	Brings Emotional Balance, Ease	Soothes Skin	Dominant, Medicinal
Ylang Ylang	Seductive, Erotic to All Senses	Energizing for Skin	Full Bodied, a Major Aphrodisiac
Petitgrain	Emotionally Balancing, Heightens Senses	Refreshing for Skin	Soft Floral, Fresh
Sandalwood	Arousing, Slightly Sedating, Sexual	Tones Skin and Hair	Woody, Spicy, Sensual
Peppermint	Cheers Spirit, Enlightens	Decongestant, Relieves Nausea and Headaches	Fresh, Cold
Sweet Pea	Brings Inner Peace, Tranquility	Soothes Tired Feet	Fresh, Floral, Smooth to Senses
Rose	Balancing, Promotes Inner Purity	Relieves Stomach Upsets, Skin Problems	Dominant Sweet Floral

Oils to Keep Handy
Almond, Cherry, Heliotrope, Lilac, Mango, Narcissus, Neroli, Peach, Violet

These can be used for scenting just about anything from pillows to lamps to water to bouquets. Also remember that essential oils are very potent. They should always be diluted with jojoba oil when using on skin. Fragrance oils are usually made to be directly applied to the skin, so make sure that you check first.

Conclusion
Seduce Yourself

Use this opportunity to become your own poet. Invent your own seductions; create your very own ideas and menus. Use a gorgeous notebook, chosen especially for the purpose. Write only in pen, for if you ever erase anything that you write, you will regret it, I promise you. Do not write as if anyone is watching or anyone cares. Now you will let the beautiful nymph inside you burst out, and glow with the power of being you, of being woman.

Be free.

Be yourself.

Seduce your own heart.

ABOUT THE AUTHOR

Snow Raven Starborn is a second-generation flower child, poet, and writer. She has written for and coedited "Coffee," a poetry newsletter distributed to coffeehouses in San Diego, where she currently resides. Visit her website at www.helpforlovers.com.